# HOW CAN YOU NOT SEE THE SIGNS?

*For Leaders to Notice the Signs of a Toxic Culture*
*For Employees to Notice Toxic Behaviour*

Jo Woodhouse

**How can you not see the signs?**
For Leaders to Notice the Signs of a Toxic Culture
For Employees to Notice Toxic Behaviour

First published in Australia by Jo Woodhouse 2024
www.jowoodhouse.com

A catalogue record for this
book is available from the
National Library of Australia

ISBN: 978-0-6459418-2-1 (pbk)
ISBN: 978-0-6459418-3-8 (ebk)

Any similarity to other persons' stories, poems or comments, living or dead, is completely unintentional and coincidental.

Typesetting and design by Publicious Book Publishing
Published in collaboration with Publicious Book Publishing
www.publicious.com.au

Edited by Julie Guthrie (Publicious)

Cover image: Publicious Book Publishing
Cover image: Lotus by Jay Castor © (Shutterstock)
Eva Campbell image and quote: Eva Campbell ©

## Dedication

Thank you to everyone who helped bring this book to life and for being part the amazing resource section.

*Special mention to the following people for reviewing and contributing in some way.*

Alexander N. Andrews: Leadership Consultant, Keynote Speaker and Author of the bestseller: *UNLIKE A BOSS*, Australia

Alison Turner PhD: Counselling Psychologist, Australia

Andy McDermott: Publicious Book Publishing Services, Australia

Donna Empson: Marketing Manager, Australia

Dr Suzanne Henwood: Director, mBraining4Success, New Zealand

Graeme Moat: Head Teacher, TAFE NSW, Australia

Jonathan Wilson: Ambassador, Stop Hurt at Work, United Kingdom

Julie Guthrie: Publicious Book Publishing Services, Australia

Karen O'Connor: General Manager/Vice President, Healthcare, Australia

Kasia Musur: Founder, VENT, Germany

Kathryn Jackson: Leadership Coach and Founder of the award-winning programme: The Great Recharge, New Zealand

Linda Crockett: Founder of The Canadian Institute of Workplace Bullying Resources, Canada

Marisa Corniola: Continuous Improvement/Transformation Professional, Australia

Mark Hughes: Machine Operator, Manufacturing, Australia

Nicki Eyre: Director, Conduct Change Ltd, United Kingdom

Traci Carse: TC Psychology, Australia

Victoria Thatcher: Head of Payroll, United Kingdom

**Alexander N. Andrews: Leadership Consultant, Keynote Speaker and author of the bestseller UNLIKE A BOSS, Australia**

How can you not see the signs? Indeed, how can you not? Simple. Over the years, workplaces have seemingly turned a blind eye and in doing so, in many of them, employees have become 'battle hardened', sadly paying forward the treatment they have been served up. All the while, others are crumbling on the inside, craving help as they are enveloped by toxic culture.

According to a University of South Australia study released in June 2021, those who work in workplaces with toxic culture are 300% more likely to develop depression. For those seeking a compelling call to action, this statistic alone should speak volumes.

In this unique and compelling resource, you'll be taken on a heartfelt journey via emotive poetry underpinned with actionable guidance on workplace bullying. You'll be compelled to answer the calls to action on your all-important workplace culture.

It's not written as an academic text requiring a dictionary to understand, but more so as a relatable text making it accessible to everyone.

With all leaders having a duty of care to their employees, can you afford not to read this book and respond appropriately? The only answer is zero tolerance for bullying.

**Dr Suzanne Henwood: Director, mBraining4Success, New Zealand**

This book is hitting the shelves at just the right time.

We are in the midst of a revolution whereby staff and employees are saying 'no more'. Bullying, incivility, toxic workplaces, and undue pressures are creating an environment that is damaging and potentially life ending. People are being damaged because they are going to work—and it has to stop.

Jo Woodhouse offers a fabulous alternative to the academic text, which hopefully will touch people at the heart—making them stand up and pay attention. This book is a call to action—a serious invitation to reflect on our own behaviour and be part of creating positive change.

This can be read by individuals to reassure them they are not alone. It can be read by teams, to open up deep conversations and discussion about what is really going on. And it can be read by leaders, to hear what staff are experiencing in the workplace.

I know I will be keeping this book close and using it with my clients, and in my trainings, to give a wide and varied perspective on what happens when work goes wrong—and what we can do to create positive change to ensure things are different in the future.

**Graeme Moat: Head Teacher, TAFE NSW, Australia**

Making mental health a top priority in the workplace is crucial for ensuring the best work from employees. This book empowers leaders to cultivate a considerate work environment with our language, time and support that we offer those we lead. As an employee, it offers advice on how to spot the signs of a toxic work environment.

Jo Woodhouse welcomes a different perspective to academic texts and articles, written in simplistic language, making it an accessible read and a perfect guide to create a mentally healthy workplace.

This book asks us to self-reflect and consider:

Is what I am asking of my employees unrealistic?
Am I setting a good example for both my employer or employee on how to treat me?
Am I doing my part to contribute to a positive working environment?

**Jonathan Wilson LLB(Hons) BA(Hons): Public Speaker, Ambassador at Stop Hurt at Work, United Kingdom**

As a leader, and having experienced bullying in the workplace, I see this book as essential reading. It's written with both thought and experience and is insightful and invaluable. It clearly voices the impact on the mind of employees familiar with bullying behaviour and helps in understanding it's not their fault.

Reflection of the words in this book will encourage those in the workplace to carefully consider how their actions may detrimentally impact the health of colleagues and the organisation.

I am hopeful it will create psychological safety in workplaces.

**Karen O'Connor: General Manager/Vice President, Healthcare, Australia**

Delve into the insightful poems by Jo Woodhouse of *How Can You Not See the Signs?* A candid insight for leaders, teams and everyone in between. It's not your typical cover-to-cover read; instead, it's a book that meets you where you are. You can easily navigate to topics that resonate, offering a different perspective on the impact of your leadership or reflecting exactly what you're feeling at that time.

As someone who has walked both as an employee in toxic cultures and as a leader trying to turn a toxic culture around, it serves as a stark reminder of the profound impact leaders can have.

This unique approach makes it a must-have companion for anyone in the leadership game. Whether you're at the helm or part of the crew, this book resonates, offering insights that hit close to home and emphasising the transformative power of leadership.

Thank you, Jo, for being brave, telling your story through poetry and creating an extraordinary piece of work.

**Kasia Musur: Founder, VENT, Germany**

There is no one way to describe the experience of working in a toxic environment. There is no one magical solution that can help every single person going through it.

This book touches on so many aspects of abuse at work, and from multiple perspectives, making it a great source for targets and for leaders who are proactively working towards preventing and reducing harm.

What better medium than poetry to express emotion and complexity of experiencing incivility.

**Kathryn Jackson: Leadership Coach & Founder of the award-winning programme: The Great Recharge. Also, a facilitator, mentor, and author, New Zealand**

Global workplaces have a challenge ahead of them. The 'COVID effect' has raised the stakes when it comes to wellbeing at work.

With a commitment to 'wellbeing' being shared on company visions, missions and values around the world, we have some uncomfortable truths ahead.

- Are we choosing the people leaders who deeply care about their teams? ... or are we simply promoting based on length of service or technical skills?

- Do our promotion and reward decisions truly celebrate health? ... or do we applaud the people who work the longest hours, and give up their holidays to achieve business goals?

- Will we be courageous enough to challenge and address some of the twenty-first century working practices that no longer serve our modern world? ... or will we continue to find excuses about which team owns the responsibility for doing this?

A difficult truth is that sometimes we don't realise that the behaviours we exhibit are contributing to toxic workplaces.

Sometimes our own batteries become so drained that whether we are a leader or an employee, we hurt the people around us.

There have been many books that highlight the positive impact of having a healthy culture at work over the years, but this is a book with a difference.

Not only does it carefully step through some of the indicators for a toxic culture (whether you're a leader or an employee), it also shares some deeply personal insights, thanks to a series of poems that call out some of the warning signs.

I defy any reader to have a dry eye by the end of 'What if I was Your Child?' It is perhaps a useful question for us all to consider during many of our conversations at work.

A great many companies already understand the importance of having a healthy culture, and for them this book will be a reminder of the reasons they are committed to this purpose. For other companies, I hope this book is a wake-up call as it enables disgruntled employees at all levels within the company to give voice to their experience at work.

**Linda Crockett: Founder of The Canadian Institute of Workplace Bullying Resources, Canada**

Survivors and thrivers of workplace psychological harassment or psychological violence (bullying in its limitless spectrum of forms) will find creative ways to share their story, release their grief and find their voice and sense of resilience once again.

The injury of workplace bullying will often leave one feeling any or all of the feelings Jo Woodhouse has described in her book. The pain of this abuse touches the soul—and the words in this book help heal it. Her words are validating, awareness building and perhaps even triggering for some, but most importantly, readers will know from this writing that Jo understands what they have been through.

There is hope for anyone. Just reach out, and know that no-one is alone.

**Nicki Eyre: Director, Conduct Change Ltd, United Kingdom**

Raising awareness about workplace bullying and the damage that it can cause to both individuals and businesses is at the heart of all my work. It can be a difficult subject to tackle, so finding a book that uses a unique approach is a breath of fresh air!

Jo has brought the subject to life through poems that prompt you to ask yourself questions that involve deep self-reflection as well as questioning leadership and the wider workplace.

Whether you read the whole book at once, or dip into different poems each day, you'll be certain to read important reminders about what is important for safe, healthy and respectful workplaces.

**Traci Carse: TC Psychology, Australia**

*How Can You Not See the Signs* is an evocative collection of poetry that delves into the particulars of toxic workplace culture.

Jo Woodhouse has successfully harnessed the power of poetry to raise awareness and invite self-reflection in readers to consider our own experiences and professional spheres, fostering a deeper understanding of what a healthy workplace culture looks like and the behaviours that contribute to this.

Simple, concise, emotive language calls out what gets in the way—bullying, disrespectful and unsupportive workplace behaviours, and the systemic conditions that underpin them.

Importantly, the book also offers practical insights for positive change. We know good work is good for people. Together, we need to proactively create the workplace cultural conditions for good work to be the norm. This book is a stark reminder for us to do just that.

# Mental health in the workplace

There is nothing more important than our mental health. And mental health in the workplace is essential. Our mental health drives everything we do. It can have a ripple effect on our work and other aspects of our life. In our work, it affects our productivity, creativity, absenteeism, conflict, projects, staff turnover, and stress levels. We need satisfaction, meaning and purpose. In our personal lives, it affects our relationships and our physical health.

We have a real problem around mental health in the workplace and there's a lot that needs to change. Many companies don't adequately prioritise mental health. They talk the talk, but don't walk the walk. And there's too much harmful behaviour.

Companies have employees who are unhappy, overwhelmed and exhausted. This creates a breeding ground for stress and anxiety. Their hard work and long hours is rewarded with more work. So many employees are experiencing burnout. They can't sleep and their health is suffering, but they keep going regardless of their own health because they have commitments and families to think about. We spend the majority of our time at work, but there's something seriously wrong when the workplace is stopping us from living life. And this in turn is making us sick. Life is precious and time is the one thing we will never get back.

Over the years, many of us have experienced toxic behaviour in the workplace. A toxic workplace can be debilitating. Not only do we deal with the ripple effect of our own mental and physical health suffering, but we also watch our colleagues suffer, where sometimes we can feel completely helpless.

When some people talk about their experiences in the workplace, they are still traumatised. Some have been so traumatised, they won't even discuss it because it triggers them so much and they don't want to relive it. It gives them so much anxiety. It can bring immediate tears to their eyes. Toxic behaviour is happening in the workplace, regardless of the company, industry or country. And that alone is frightening.

And the terrifying reality is that in some cases, people have tried to take their own life, or thought about it, because they feel they cannot handle it. The fact is they may already be dealing with so much. Their mental and physical health may have been affected by way of stress, gaslighting, anxiety, abuse, blame, having extensive workloads, or a combination of all the above—none of which are healthy. They could be triggered by past experiences or live with a mental illness themselves. The workplace can also be the start of mental health issues if it's serious enough. We all agree to work for a company for pay and benefits, not abuse. The workplace should be safe and should not make anyone think about wanting to end their life. But the reality is, it can absolutely be a work scenario that is the tipping point for someone to take their own life!

I ask that when you read this book, you dig deep and think very carefully about your own actions. As a 'leader', how have you treated employees? How have you made them feel? What type of culture does your company have? Have you ever dug deep enough to see what it really looks like, and not just what you think it looks like? Some 'leaders' out there need to realise that they are part of the problem and their behaviour can be very obvious to other people, even if they don't see it themselves. If you treat people in a toxic way, you're not a leader at all and you don't have the respect of your team. You might think you do, but I can assure you, you don't!

Mental health conditions are real and are a significant and growing concern in the workplace. It's so important to take action to ensure your organisation is able to **prevent, support and respond** to mental health risks. Creating a safe, supportive and inclusive work environment, where mental health is openly discussed and addressed, is critical for nurturing a healthy and productive workforce.

The purpose of this book is to understand different types of cultures and behaviours and what that means for an employee's mental health. Some people may not even realise the impact of their own behaviour or the consequences of their actions. If someone is spiralling, the person who contributed to this spiral may be going about their day, completely oblivious to the impact their behaviour has had on someone else's life. It also highlights the behaviour so employees can see that maybe the way they are being treated is not right and shouldn't be acceptable. In some companies, there are multiple culprits causing multiple bouts of pain.

I also share how together we can make change and create a positive and caring culture, where everyone feels safe, seen, heard, respected, appreciated, and included.

With positive change and kindness, we can create a successful, safe, happy, and healthy environment for everyone. That's all employees want—to stop all the toxic and negative behaviour, and to work for a company they can trust and feel like they belong in. And every employee deserves that. Remember, every person has a life outside of work. They have a partner, a family, friends, hobbies, interests, and maybe they've been through serious scenarios in life. They could also be dealing with serious issues or illness. Time shouldn't be taken away from them due to workplace bullying or unrealistic workloads taking its toll on employees and their mental and physical health. Life is just too short!

I hope this book highlights the dangers currently in the workplace and brings change in some way. By creating great leaders, who then create great leaders, together we can build a safe and successful workplace for everyone. And remember, anyone can be a leader in the company without actually being in the leadership team. It's all about stepping up, learning and making positive change.

By the way, I'm not putting every company in this bucket because I do know there are some great companies out there, who do focus on a positive company culture. There are also great leaders, and I have had the privilege and honour of working with some of them over the years.

Why not make it your company goal to become a company of choice, where everyone wants to come and work, and candidates are knocking down your door for the opportunity? How good would that be for your company?

## *Change the way your people are managed!*

Gallup is a global analytics and advisory company founded in 1935 by George Gallup, a pioneer in public opinion research.

Gallup is renowned for its public opinion polls, which gauge public sentiment on a wide range of issues, from political preferences to social trends. The Gallup Poll, launched in 1935, is one of the most respected and widely cited polls in the world.

In the State of the Global Workplace 2023 Report, Gallup has found one clear answer: **Change the way your people are managed.**

In this year's State of the Global Workplace Report, Gallup estimates that low engagement costs the global economy $8.8 trillion. That's 9% of global GDP — enough to make the difference between success and a failure for humanity.

*Poor management leads to lost customers and lost profits, but it also leads to miserable lives.* Gallup's research into wellbeing at work finds that having a job you hate is worse than being unemployed — and those negative emotions end up at home, impacting relationships with family.

If you're not thriving at work, you're unlikely to be thriving at life.

More information can be found at www.gallup.com

# Table of Contents

## WHAT DOES NOT HAVING A GOOD CULTURAL FIT MEAN?

Not having a good cultural fit will absolutely set your company up to fail. If there is an unclear vision or company direction, if staff members aren't working together as a team, if there are office politics, bullying or blaming cultures, if there are unclear expectations, if there is a 'boys' club', if there is a high turnover of staff—the company is already on the path to failure.

Allowing a toxic culture to run through the organisation and not creating a positive culture of trust, respect, learning, and growth would set any company up to fail. Employees will follow the behaviour of their leaders, so a toxic culture will trickle through the organisation as normal, acceptable behaviour.

One of the main warning signs of a toxic culture is a high turnover of staff. When so many staff members are leaving, this is a major red flag. Staff don't leave a happy and healthy culture; they leave poor leadership or poor managers.

It might take employees a long time to leave a toxic company because they just don't have the energy to go through the process. They're stressed, exhausted, their health is suffering, they've lost their confidence. They will not be showing their best self to a potential new employer. So they will continue to struggle in an unhealthy environment.

However, having employees who are abused, deflated, disappointed, and burnt out is not going to help a company to grow either. They will not be able to perform at their best—physically or mentally—to ensure the best outcomes for the company or your customers.

How can you not see the signs that this may be happening in your company? As a 'leader', how can you not see what is actually happening on your watch? A leader, or leaders, may also be a bully; however, if this is the case, they are not a leader, they just have the title. Because remember, a true leader is not a bully at all.

Sometimes, the toxicity has been going on for so long, it's accepted as normal behaviour. Some employees may have been bullied for some time and may not even realise it. Other times, bullying is so obvious to many, but nobody is willing to speak up.

## Let's make a difference

We can no longer suffer in silence
We need to speak up and be heard
To demand change within the workplace
Right now there's no reward

We deserve a safe environment
We deserve respect and dignity
We need to change toxic behaviour
We're drowning in negativity

What happened to old-fashioned values
And treating each other with respect
Showing kindness to one another
While working with caring and with ethics?

There are millions of people who suffer
And they're just trying to survive
The toxic workplace they're employed in
Some are trying to stay alive

This is no good for your company
And it won't help you grow
It will hold you back and cost you
Can you see what it really shows?

Please take what you read here seriously
Your employees' lives could be at stake
Please ensure that you protect them
For the difference you can make

We must get serious about mental health
And it's very clear to see
The workplace is so unhealthy
And prevention is the key

We need to all stand up together
And say 'No' to this bullying beast
No longer will we accept it
So together let's make a difference

## Can someone tell me why?

We all get up and go to work each day
We have bills and families
But there's toxicity in the workplace
And no-one seems to be at ease

Staff just want to come to work each day
And do the best they can
Doing the right thing for the company
And where possible, lend a hand

But why do people have an ego?
Why do they treat their team so bad?
No way is it acceptable
And I just don't understand

What's with this toxic culture
Of bullying or blame
Of lying and accusations?
There's no need for this game

Do some think it gives them power
Or think that's how to lead a team?
I can assure you that it isn't
As this behaviour is extreme

Why do some continually victimise
Or constantly harass?
It so damaging to others
And it needs to be addressed

There's no need for all this chaos
For the suffering and the pain
And you don't see the outcome
When you play this dangerous game

All this bullying can result in trauma
It can manifest in different ways
Causing anxiety, depression and PTSD
Making your staff struggle through the day

The effects can be long lasting
And have an impact on someone's life
Affecting sleep and socialisation
Putting your employee in such strife

Don't think you haven't hurt them
Because you didn't raise your hand
This is psychological abuse
So make sure you understand

Some employees are beaten so far down
It affects all parts of their life
So much so they've thought about
If they should take their life

Employees may need ongoing counselling
Which they may struggle to afford
Adding financial pressure to their issues
This really cannot be ignored

So, if toxic is your culture
And it seems no rules apply
If it's acceptable behaviour
Can someone tell me why?

### *A toxic workplace is like poison*

A toxic workplace is like poison
It will spread if not contained
It can make your employees very sick
So ensure it's decimated

If poison runs throughout your workplace
It'll deprive oxygen in your team
It will block all motivation
And company-wide prestige

It will increase employees' heart rates
Breathing and body temperatures
As they're dealing with anxiety
And other pain this may endure

You'll never be successful
With poison running through your team
It will continually kill your progress
And your employees' self-esteem

Some poisons may not be very potent
Causing problems with prolonged exposure
Other poisons are so potent
You need to find a strong enclosure

There's no place for poison in the workplace
So keep the bad behaviours out
Lock away all toxic cultures
And take away the fear of doubt

## The interview process

Through the interview process, the company usually promotes a healthy or positive culture and candidates join the company, partly for this reason. For some candidates, a positive culture is the main reason to actually join the company, especially if they have had previous bad experiences. One of the worst things an employee can do is leave a toxic work environment, only to end up in another one. This can create ongoing issues for them.

When the employee commences work, they are excited for the new opportunities or innovation. The have the ability to collaborate with new teammates and try to make a difference, only to find that there is a blaming, bullying or toxic theme. This is not what was sold to them. This was not what they signed up for. This is not what they agreed to.

Candidates feel disappointed, annoyed and ripped off if they are sold a professional company during the interview process and it's not what they end up receiving. This has a direct effect on an employee's mental health. It could be triggering a past experience, they may require counselling and it can be a major setback for their own career.

Please ensure you deliver the culture you promise your candidates in the interview process. This is the beginning of you being the company an employee can trust.

## *My employment contract did not state*

*Expected behaviour:*

You may be gaslit
You may be lied to
You may be bullied
You may be accused
You may be harassed
You may be excluded
You may be disrespected
You may become a victim
You may be sexually harassed
You may be discriminated against
You may be blamed for someone else's bad decision or things you didn't do
You may raise serious concerns with management, only to have them dismissed
You may work late at night and over weekends to cover an unrealistic workload, unrealistic expectations or because the goal posts will constantly move

Sign here: _____

No employment contract incorporates this kind of behaviour.

If your company treats employees this way, add this as a clause to your employment contracts and see how many new employees sign it.

I don't believe anyone would sign this contract and agree to this behaviour. So, why is it so prevalent in the workplace?

Companies have a legal responsibility to provide a safe work environment, both mentally and physically. The best way to do that is to prevent issues in the first place.

There are very clear standards around implementing physical safety protocols in the workplace to help prevent risk or accidents. For example, there are techniques on how to lift things safely, preventative measures for trip hazards, equipment practices, lighting, and electricity practices.

We need to ensure we have the same very clear, preventative measures and standards around mental health in the workplace. This should include a zero tolerance for bullying. Ensure there are standards in your workplace to communicate that bullying and toxicity will not be tolerated and there will be consequences for employees, on any level, who practice this behaviour.

But companies can't just tick a box and 'talk the talk', they need to actually follow through and 'walk the walk', making it a priority in the company and ensuring there are no repercussions if an employee speaks up in the workplace.

## *You are the CEO*

You are the CEO of your company
The highest leader of your team
How will you set up your leadership
To ensure everyone succeeds?

Will you set high expectations?
Have ongoing training for your staff?
Will you ensure they have resources?
Will you be there when they ask?

Will you ensure old-fashioned values
Like treating others with respect
Of having trust and honesty
For your leaders to be the best?

How will you support if staff are failing
Or going through some troubled times?
Sometimes life is overwhelming
Can you even see the signs?

Will you raise awareness on mental health
And teach your team to read the signs?
Will you bring in the expert trainers
And build their skillsets over time?

Do you even know what to look out for
If staff are struggling mentally?
Will you personally reach out to them
And help them through with empathy?

Will you change the way of workloads?
It seems unrealistic hours is the norm
The expectation that staff will continue to work
From dusk until the dawn

Not ensuring a positive culture
Is setting your business up to fail
Toxicity breeds within the workplace
Making it impossible to prevail

Toxic cultures damage employees
They can cause pain for many years
They may require ongoing counselling
They may result in ongoing fears

You earn respect through your own actions
Not with words you throw about
Leading with your own behaviour
Will make your leadership stand out

You need to set the corporate values
Drive your strategy and growth
Represent us to our stakeholders
What will be your best approach?

You want to tell stakeholders a good story
And report a business that shows growth
But you can't do that with a toxic culture
It might also leave you exposed

You need to give your team a purpose
A direction to help them through the day
So if they're facing challenges
You can help show them the way

Teams with a purpose tend to be happier
They have increased resilience
They have a greater sense of fulfilment
And feel they make a difference

So, remember your team are watching
For the leadership you'll show
They will follow in your footsteps
Because you are the CEO

## *Leadership is about your employees*

A leader is not just a title
It's something developed over time
You need to grow your skillset
So your leadership will shine

It's a vast responsibility
Dealing with difficult situations
You need to make the hard decisions
There can be so many frustrations

Being a leader can be rewarding
As you watch your employees grow
If you guide with trust and understanding
You can reap the seeds you sow

Do you give clear vision of the company
And a purpose for your team?
Do you inspire to work towards a goal
Or is staff lacking self-esteem?

Have you inspired your team to walk with you
To take this journey side by side?
Or are you just giving them direction
Without their knowledge of the ride?

Do you go against your corporate values?
They should be led from the top
Do you even practice what you preach
If not, then what's the point?

Do you have good communication
Or do you scream and shout?
Do you set clear expectations
And calm their minds of doubt?

Do you make good decisions
Or are some pretty poor?
Do you take accountability
If employees are heading for the door?

Do you ensure your teams are notified
Of issues raised in management meetings?
Keeping communication open
So everyone understands the situation

There's nothing more frustrating
When there's problems or issues raised
But communication's broken
And others are then blamed

Do you really hear what staff are saying
Or do you leave them facing doubt?
Is there too much constant chaos?
Do your customers want out?

Do you create a positive environment?
Are staff respected and embraced?
Do you lead by your own example?
What type of energy do you portray?

Do you appreciate or value staff?
Do you have empathy?
Do you have positive relationships?
Is there a sense of community?

If you're the leader of this team
Do you have your staff's respect?
Because employees are watching closely
At the behaviour you project

Is your energy so contagious?
The team just want to be around you
When you always show good character
They see what they can aspire to

A leader needs to coach and guide
They inspire their employees
They help with career progression
And they motivate their teams

Have you taught your staff key lessons
Or have you taught them what not to do?
What is your purpose to your team?
What do they really learn from you?

Have you trained to be a leader?
Have you trained to manage staff?
Many people take positions
Without the knowledge for the task

Have *you* ensured *your team* is qualified?
Are they trained to manage staff?
Can you *guarantee* these leaders
Have the right skills for this task?

Leadership is not all about the numbers
Without a solid team they'll never grow
It's the team that make the difference
For the results you want to show

How you treat staff will last a lifetime
What will be your legacy?
How do you want them to remember you
As a leader or enemy?

There is one vital element
It seems not everybody sees
But it's the most important one
Leadership is about your employees!

## Are you killing your company brand?

Toxic leaders impact a company name
And damage the company brand
When a company has high staff turnover
Remaining staff don't understand

Toxic leaders affect company branding
When the word upon the street
Is a toxic and bullying culture
Where many staff have found defeat

Toxic leaders harm client relationships
Clients won't want to deal with them
Customers no longer have their loyalty
As they build relationships again

Toxic leaders damage your reputation
As they make poor decisions
Which can lead to loss of business
Employees are working in hard conditions

Toxic leaders make hiring difficult
Staff want a positive culture at work
It's hard to attract and retain good talent
With poor feedback candidates heard

Toxic leaders forget staff are their assets
They can have years of expertise
They can have first class experience
But they force good staff to leave

Past employees don't talk about 'leaders'
They talk of the company name
I couldn't stand working for that company
It's a culture of blame and shame

When employees constantly leave your company due to a toxic culture and a poor experience, it's natural that they will talk about it with friends, family, psychologists, counsellors, and potential employers.

They will also potentially add negative feedback in exit platforms like Glassdoor. More and more candidates are using platforms like Glassdoor to do their own due diligence on companies, so it acts as a warning sign for them not to join your company.

This all contributes to damaging your company brand as the conversation around your company name is constantly negative.

### The blame culture

The blame culture shows weak leadership
And it comes right from the top
It's a game of finger pointing
It's a game that should be stopped

The blame culture is so toxic
When there's someone else to blame
No-one takes responsibility
It's a constant game of blame and shame

There is endless finger pointing
It's always someone else's fault
It can create a lethal culture
It can leave the team distraught

No-one is ever responsible
For their own actions or mistakes
They hide behind another person
They do whatever it takes

The blame culture is destructive
In fact, it's dangerous!
No good can ever come from it
It's cowardly and malicious

The blame culture loses trust
And causes conflict in the team
It has many negative consequences
If staff are always being blamed

The blame culture has no winners
As employees lose all respect
So own up and be accountable
For your actions and mistakes

The blaming trickles through the company
When it's seen coming from the top
Becoming acceptable behaviour
Because the blaming never stops

The blame culture can be deadly
If someone's blamed when not at fault
It can absolutely be the final straw
For one struggling with their mental health

## How the blame culture affects an employee's mental health

No good can come from a blame culture. The blame culture is destructive and dangerous. Being employed in a blame culture can cause high stress and mental health concerns for employees.

It's not uncommon for employees to experience mental health issues due to dealing with a blame culture environment. The blame culture can actually ruin lives. It can cause long-term pain and ongoing depression, anxiety and PTSD.

The blame culture is exhausting and kills a person's self-esteem, *especially* when they are blamed for things they didn't do. If someone is already struggling with their mental health and are then blamed for something they didn't do, this can potentially be the trigger for someone to take their own life.

Some people require ongoing counselling due to this culture, which they have to pay for themselves. This can also put an extra financial burden on the person, which then becomes a further issue for them.

If you're struggling with any aspect of your work environment, consider contacting your doctor or a therapist for guidance. There are many resources available, such as hotlines, support groups and mental health professionals, that can provide support and guidance.

Remember, you are not alone and there is hope for healing and recovery.

## *The fear culture*

A fear culture is an environment
Where staff are scared to make mistakes
They're too frightened to speak up
As they're fearful of the stakes

Staff fear being publicly shamed
They fear being at fault
They don't feel valued or respected
They can fear verbal assault

Staff may walk on eggshells
They don't want to make a sound
In case they make the wrong decision
And the hands go banging down

Creativity is halted
No-one wants to make a move
With the continuous fear of being judged
For the constant disapprove

Staff won't share ideas or opinions
Even if they are valuable
They're too scared to take a risk
Which also causes low morale

This behaviour has negative consequences
With reduced productivity
There's much less innovation
Increased stress and anxiety

This is a toxic culture
Where fear will run supreme
It can be very detrimental
To mental health and company dreams

## *The silo culture*

The silo culture works independently
They don't collaborate
They don't communicate with each other
No-one seems to cooperate

There's a constant duplication
Wasting time and wasting resources
With teams working on similar projects
Instead of joining forces

There's inefficiency in the workplace
It's tough to streamline any workflows
This leads to lost productivity
And may leave the company exposed

There are communication problems
As departments work alone
Causing conflict and misunderstanding
This behaviour is well-known

It makes it difficult for your customers
Because the service that you bring
Is not a constant experience
And no-one's working as a team

## The unrealistic work expectations culture

Unrealistic work expectations
Can be impossible to meet
They can cause so much frustration
And affect the entire team

They cause stress and anxiety
Working these unrealistic hours
Causing physical and mental health issues
With decreased output and morale

It can lead to poor work quality
As staff are likely to make mistakes
When they're working such long hours
Without the adequate breaks

Staff don't have time to be creative
There's no time for innovation
There's no development for employees
And no growth for the organisation

It causes high turnover
As this pace you can't sustain
Due to the constant worker burnout
It's hard to find staff to retain

Staff aren't focusing on their priorities
Which should be their health and family
Because they're working extra hours
They don't have much time to breathe

It has an effect on customers
As staff are not always at their best
Customers suffer with poor service
Which will cause a ripple effect

## The toxic culture

If this company could see their own behaviour
And how toxic it can be
Just take one step back and think about
The way you treat your team

I wish you realised how you talk to staff
And how you think you're always right
You're always trying to test their knowledge
And you just love to call them out

There are some constant gaslighters
And they've made staff feel so small
They've made them question their ability
Or if they should be here at all!

Can you even see what you are doing
Or are you too engrossed
In thinking you have such power
And don't see what you provoke?

They blame the team when things go wrong
Even when the decision was one they made
They rarely listen to their team's input
And teams often feel betrayed

Staff aren't comfortable working with you
They always have to watch their back
They have lost respect and trust in you
Because they feel under attack

Would you want your child being bullied
And working in constant fear
In a place you could not protect them
And couldn't wipe away their tears?

Managers also experience bullying
They're belittled in front of their peers
They are laughed at for their suggestions
Some also work in constant fear

So understand management can be a victim
It's not always passed down from the top
This behaviour can come from employees
And all this behaviour needs to STOP!

## The micromanager

The micromanager is controlling
As they watch our every move
They're always hovering over us
And criticising what we do

The micromanager is demanding
We may not do things to your style
We may actually know a better way
That doesn't take up so much time

The micromanager is frustrating
Their way isn't always right
We might be going back to basics
When I've done this job all my life!

The micromanager is overbearing
They micromanage every task
Making us feel worthless
And like we can't do what we're asked

The micromanager lacks trust in their team
They don't think we can do our work
They can't see that we are capable
And it drives the team berserk

It causes high turnover
As staff look for a positive change
They feel they're not supported
Making it hard to find staff and retain

The micromanager is degrading
And it has a ripple effect
Because if they can't trust us to do our job
There's clearly no respect

## The 'boys' club'

The 'boys' club' is an informal network
And it's so very clear to see
They all support each other
And not necessarily you and me

The 'boys' club' damages the workplace
Leading to many negative moments
Including the company's reputation
And attracting or retaining talent

The 'boys' club' has been around for many years
Telling each other what to say
Protecting one another
When other staff members have to pay

The 'boys' club' can create discrimination
For women or other groups
They may be denied opportunities
Or even faced with harassment

The 'boys' club' shares common interests
They help advance each other's careers
They create exclusion and isolation
And have the staff in tears

The 'boys' club' causes low productivity
And low morale within the team
Employees are less likely to be engaged in work
As they feel excluded from the team

The 'boys' club' clearly protects each other
When staff raise issues or their hand
They tell us to work together
But they won't care to understand

The 'boys' club' is never at fault for what they do
They think their behaviour is okay
As staff members constantly suffer
As they deal with this mess each day

The 'boys' club' keeps information to themselves
They don't share it with the team
Then call you out that you don't know your job
When the issues become extreme

The 'boys' club' thinks that staff can't see
The damage that they do
As they keep backing up each other
Instead of properly following through

The 'boys' club' has a negative impact
On company culture and its values
Creating fear and intimidation
And shows employees just aren't valued

The 'boys' club' should be disabled
For the damage they do each day
Step up and be a leader
For this toxic chaos to go away

## The imposter leader

You've heard of, 'fake it till you make it'
That's what an imposter leader is about
Being in leadership positions
Hoping they won't be caught out

They have a fear of being exposed
And they hide behind their mask
Like micromanaging or scapegoating
'Cause they don't have the right skills for this task

Imposters are often interfering
They take credit for others' work
They don't know how to empower teams
They're scared of being found to be a fraud

Imposters are always on your case
You might feel there is no trust
They're experienced in controlling
Because your every move is watched

Imposters cause many issues for your company
Low productivity and low morale
It increases your staff turnover
For decisions made with no rationale

So clear out imposter leaders
Or give them the training that they need
It should be part of their development
For your business to succeed

## How toxic cultures affect an employee's mental health

Being employed in a toxic work environment can cause stress and mental health concerns.

It's not uncommon for employees to experience mental health issues due to dealing with terrible manager/s or toxic work environments. Toxic behaviour can actually ruin lives. It can cause long-term pain and ongoing depression, anxiety and PTSD. Others might turn to drinking or other addictions, which can cause a further ripple effect of issues. Moving from one toxic culture to another toxic culture will continue to compound the problem and the situation will worsen.

A toxic culture can have long-lasting effects on employees. They need time for their physical and mental health to recover. They may have lost their confidence, they may have issues with being able to trust and build new connections in a new environment, and they may have a fear of rejection if they have received constant disapproval. And the most passionate employees can lose their spark and struggle to get it back.

Some employees require ongoing counselling due to workplace bullying, which they have to pay for themselves. This can also put an extra financial burden on the employee.

Employees may have had a toxic personal relationship that was very traumatic and they had to leave. If there is ongoing toxic behaviour in the workplace, it may be causing triggers from their past experience, which could be detrimental to their health.

The toxicity can also set someone's career path backwards. If they are not getting the support they need, or they're too busy dealing with the negative environment instead of their work and development path, they may have wasted years of their career time.

Employees can also lose so much from the strain, including time due to excessive workloads. Time is the one thing you can never get back. They may not get paid for all those hours they are expected to work, so they lose personal time and they lose financially.

If you're struggling with any aspect of your work environment, consider contacting your doctor or a therapist for guidance. There are many resources available, such as hotlines, support groups and mental health professionals, that can provide support and guidance.

Remember, you are not alone and there is hope for healing and recovery.

## *Feedback from a toxic culture*

The following are comments from people who have endured a toxic culture in the workplace, and the danger it caused them. Just like these examples, there would be so many more. The workplace should NOT cause mental health issues or make someone contemplate taking their own life.

"I said goodbye to this culture
But still live with the pain
The PTSD and anxiety
Feels like it will always remain"

*"I had to leave this company
It kept triggering my past
As I watched this blaming culture
Someone was bound to take their life"*

"This job kept me awake at night
And made me suicidal
I kept thinking how and when
So, leaving this job was vital"

*"This particular day was unbearable
It made me spiral so far down
I couldn't get back up again
I didn't want to be around*

*Late that night, I'd had enough
I knew I was in strife
They made me feel like I was nothing
And I tried to take my life"*

"I was so tired from all the bullying
I was sick of the yelling – it's triggering my past relationship that I
had to get away from
The constant stress and long hours
Why am I working so hard for a company that doesn't care about me
I've never been so disrespected in my working life
Nothing was good enough
I've never been made to feel so small
I started questioning my ability
Maybe they're right
Maybe I can't do this
Maybe I am stupid
Maybe it's easier if I wasn't here at all"

## *The narcissist*

A narcissist inflates their own importance
Needing superiority and respect
They have a lack of empathy
And create unhealthy environments

Do you understand a narcissist?
They will bully endlessly
They wouldn't care about someone's feelings
And they twist reality

A narcissist is exhausting
They need an endless supply
Of attention, abuse and drama
Sucking the life out of you and I

They will take credit for the work that's done
By other employees
Which is so very demoralising
And doesn't put our minds at ease

They set unrealistic expectations
Demand perfection, nothing less
Causing stress and anxiety for everyone
As staff try to perform their best

They will tarnish your good image
Turning other employees against you
Destroying your social network
And the good work that you do

They will also raise supporters
Manipulating others to take their side
Believing fabricated stories
Who then come along for this ride

The victim is constantly traumatised
As they are now retargeted within the team
Cycling through more abuse
And losing their self-esteem

A narcissist is micromanaging
Staff are constantly interrupted
Being criticised for even a minor mistake
Staff don't feel like they are trusted

They will constantly harass you
They will make you feel so small
They'll undermine your credibility
Somehow, they'll seem so sure

Even if you're doing all you can
It will never be good enough
Because they'll keep coming at you
Working with them is so tough

You might talk to other colleagues
They may see what's going on
But they'll be far too scared to intervene
They'll sit back and just look on

The narcissist won't care what you're dealing with
They won't even care to know
They'll be preoccupied with power
And not what might be going on at home

They may gaslight their employees
Make them question their sanity
Or their perception of reality
Causing employee's agony

They bring down other people
Even one's that are their mates
And talk about them behind their backs
Others can see how this translates

They can't see their own reflection
There's nothing wrong with what they do
But they see fault in your reaction
'Cause every issue's caused by you!

They'll make themselves to be the victim
They'll tell lies and they'll twist truths
They'll say, you are in fact the villain
And that there's been no abuse

This behaviour is so dangerous
And it can put employees in such strife
It can make staff spiral and think about
If they should take their life!

## How the narcissist affects an employee's mental health

Working with narcissistic behaviours can lead to various negative consequences and definitely cause stress and mental health concerns.

Narcissists are also hard to identify in the beginning as they can often be extremely charming and engaging, so when the behaviour or attitude flips, it can come as a shock and people often wonder why they didn't see it.

Working with a narcissistic manager creates a very stressful working environment. This can lead to heightened anxiety within the team. Their constant demands, lack of empathy and unrealistic expectations can leave employees feeling overwhelmed and on edge. This can also lead to burnout and exhaustion as employees are emotionally depleted and unable to cope with their demanding job.

Working with this constant stress and anxiety caused by this environment can lead to depression and in some cases, suicide. The stress spills over into their personal lives and affects all of their relationships, causing them to become emotionally unavailable, withdrawn and irritable. This can cause further tension in their personal relationships. The employee will also lack motivation and engagement as they feel undervalued and disengaged.

With a narcissist's constant criticising and belittling, they lower a person's confidence and self-esteem, making people doubt their own ability and self-worth. It can also make it difficult for a person to form healthy relationships, achieve their goals and live an enjoyable life.

Some people may have left a personal relationship due to narcissistic behaviour. Reliving this behaviour in the workplace could be triggering past trauma, which could be very dangerous.

If you are experiencing this behaviour, it is crucial to seek help.

If you're struggling with any aspect of your work environment, consider contacting your doctor or a therapist for guidance. There are many resources available, such as hotlines, support groups and mental health professionals, that can provide support and guidance.

Remember, you are not alone and there is hope for healing and recovery.

## The gaslighter

A gaslighter manipulates another
Into questioning their own sanity
Or their perception of reality
By distorting facts so easily

A gaslighter can break your spirit
Destroying hope and self-esteem
Abuse, control and manipulation
Can take so long to heal

Why do you twist my words around?
Or make me doubt myself?
Why do you make me feel I'm worthless?
It says so much about yourself

You say, 'I didn't say things'
When I clearly know I did
Or that I imagined something
You speak to me like I'm stupid!

You tell me that I'm sensitive
Or you lie when I have proof
You tell me that I make things up
And make me doubt myself

You blame me when it's your mistake
You then make me feel ashamed
You make me feel like I'm a burden
I'm so tired of being blamed

You're always trying to control me
And make me feel I can't do my job
I now question my ability
This behaviour needs to stop!

Does it make you feel important
Even if it shows that you are small?
You make me feel I'm going crazy
And you don't care at all

Do you even know what you are doing
Or what this behaviour can initiate?
Do you know how it's debilitating
And that it can end in fate?

Gaslighting is a form of abuse
No-one signs up for this
It's not in our agreements
And it's such torture in itself

This behaviour should have implications
They should never lead a team
A gaslighter is not a leader
And repercussions should be extreme

Gaslighters are so toxic
And this behaviour is a worry
Because it causes low self-esteem
Depression and anxiety

This behaviour is so dangerous
And it can put people in such strife
It can make staff spiral and think about
If they should take their life!

## How the gaslighter affects an employee's mental health

Working with gaslighting behaviours can definitely cause stress and mental health concerns.

When you break someone down, you are breaking them psychologically, mentally and emotionally. It can have a devastating effect on a person's mental and emotional well-being. Employees are manipulated into doubting their own perception, memories and sanity. This can make employees question their own judgement and hinder their ability to perform well and do their job.

Gaslighting leaves employees in a state of confusion, leaving them feeling anxious and disorientated as they question their own experiences and realities. This leads to further stress and anxiety. The constant gaslighting undermines an employee's confidence and self-esteem, leaving them feeling worthless and inadequate.

Many people suffer from stress, nervousness, insomnia, fatigue, anxiety, depression, post-traumatic stress disorder, and in some cases, suicidal thoughts. It can also make it difficult for a person to form healthy relationships, achieve their goals and live an enjoyable life.

Some people may have left a personal relationship due to gaslighting behaviour. Reliving this behaviour in the workplace could be triggering past trauma, which could be very dangerous.

If you are experiencing this behaviour, it is crucial to seek help.

If you're struggling with any aspect of your work environment, consider contacting your doctor or a therapist for guidance. There are many resources available, such as hotlines, support groups and mental health professionals, that can provide support and guidance.

Remember, you are not alone and there is hope for healing and recovery.

# What if I was your child?

What if I was your child
Who struggled with their mental health?
Knowing what I'd already been through
And the pain and fear I'd felt

What if I was your child
And already tried to take my life?
And I'm fighting with everything I have
To move forward with my life

What if I was your child
And my workplace became my hell?
It didn't help with my recovery
And in fact, it helped me spiral

What if I was your child
Would you want someone protecting me?
Instead of making my life harder
Than it already had to be

What if I was your child
Would you want someone abusing me?
Someone who treated me with disrespect
Making me feel *sadness*

What if I was your child
Would you want someone blaming me?
For something that I didn't do
Making me feel *shamed*

What if I was your child
Would you want someone screaming at me?
When presenting the hours of work I've done
Making me *worthless*

What if I was your child
Would you want someone harassing me?
And never thinking to let up
Making me feel *fatigued*

What if I was your child
And I had nothing left to give?
Because this workplace took it all from me
Including my strength to live

What if you were my manager
And I actually took my life?
And you now had to live with that
How would you move on with life?

## *I live with depression*

I live with depression
And I struggle constantly
I force myself to get out of bed to face the day
I put on a brave face and hide behind my mask
As I get to work, I feel the sharks circling me
I'm sometimes harassed for information
immediately that takes weeks to collate
Or I'm blamed for something I didn't do
Management call me out it in front of my colleagues
These are the actions that make me feel small
Why do they have to treat me like this?
It's not necessary
My life is hard enough
It makes me spiral
I just need to get through this day
And hopefully the next and the next...

### *How can you not see the signs?*
### *- Leader*

How can you not see the signs
If so many staff want out?
If there's so many staff resigning
Leaving the ones behind in doubt

Have you asked yourself this question?
What's changed so much to leave?
Is it toxicity and burnout
Or is it because of poor leadership?

Do you know how your staff are struggling
Or if they feel worthless or alone?
Do you know how hard they work for you
And fall apart when they get home?

Do you speak directly to your staff
To find out how they feel?
And really listen to the answers
Do you help your staff to heal?

Do you blame COVID for staff turnover?
Do you know that's an excuse?
It's not COVID's fault staff are leaving
It might be due to much abuse

Do you think, 'the great resignation'
Has a part to play?
It plays no part in how staff are treated
And what they're faced with every day

Do you really want to know the answers
So you can make a positive change
And ensure staff a work/life balance
For everyone to re-engage?

This is the company you are leading
Make the change for better times
Or a toxic legacy is what you'll leave behind
How can you not see the signs?

## *How can you not see the signs?*
## *- Employee*

How can you not see the signs
If you're not treated well
If your manager is abusive
Putting you under their spell?

How can you not see the signs
If so many staff are leaving?
Doesn't this tell you something's wrong?
What are you perceiving?

How can you not see the signs?
You know how they make you feel
They don't listen when you're talking
Look at what you could reveal?

How can you not see the signs
If you're working all the time
If you work in constant chaos
With direction changing all the time?

How can you not see the signs?
You should be treated with respect
With trust and care and empathy
And not with such neglect

How can you not see the signs?
This culture needs to change
This behaviour is so toxic
And the team is not engaged

Speak up or get out of this workplace
Look hard and you will see
You're working in toxicity
It's not a healthy place to be

This is the culture you're employed in
But your health may be in decline
Should you stay within this company?
How can you not see the signs?

## *Quietly quitting*

Have you noticed staff quietly quitting?
Do you understand what that means?
They don't have the energy to give it their all anymore
And they may have low self-esteem

They only work the minimum hours
And do the minimum amount of work
They don't take on any new projects
And have a disconnection with their work

Employees feel undervalued
They feel overworked and underpaid
This is a very real trend in the market
And it leaves staff disengaged

When an employee quietly quits
It has an impact on the role
They may have unfinished projects
Where other staff need to be enrolled

It may damage their relationships
With managers and employees
Making it hard for them to trust again
Causing further issues in the team

This leads to no job satisfaction
It doesn't help anyone's career
It damages the company's reputation
And staff soon disappear

If staff have chosen to leave the company
And they switch off in that time
They may not do a proper handover
Which causes further issues down the line

## Dysregulation in the workplace

Dysregulation is a state of being
A system might not be functioning as it should
Referring to a variety of contexts
The mind, body and social systems

The mind could be emotional or behavioural
The body hormonal or neurological
And when we talk about social systems, its
Social unrest, economic and political

This can manifest in the workplace
With emotional outbursts
There could be impulsive behaviours
Or conflict with colleagues and customers

Staff could have trouble controlling their anger
And also make some poor decisions
They may not be able to meet their deadlines
And struggle to control their own frustrations

What causes this in the workplace?
Personal stresses, or substance abuse
Staff may have mental health conditions
Or a toxic environment that won't defuse

What does all this mean in the workplace?
Emotions may be running high
It may not be someone's normal behaviour
It's treated with medications, diet or exercise

The world is struggling with dysregulation
Political, environmental and social concerns
Mental health is a growing problem
With stress, anxiety and depression confirmed

We're having extreme weather conditions
And the rising cost of living
There's an amplified rise of violence
And these current challenges are unforgiving

## Do you know what the end might mean?

When staff tell you there are issues
When they tell you things aren't right
Do you just tell them to work together?
Does this keep them up at night?

Are you really listening to them?
Have you lost good staff along the way?
If no-one is really hearing staff
Why would they want to stay?

You are the leaders of your team
You're the ones in whom staff trust
But have you really been supportive
In protecting all your staff?

Have you really taken seriously
The concerns the staff have raised
If they're a toxic, blaming culture
That keeps building day to day?

How can staff work together?
If they've lost respect and trust
If they constantly look behind them
As they're thrown under the bus!

Do you tell staff to work together?
But then don't do the same
And then when things don't go to plan
Is there always someone else to blame?

Do staff raise concerns directly to you?
Does it fall upon deaf ears?
Were they given the support they needed?
Were they listened to by their peers?

Remember, you are their leadership
Remember, you're a team
But if you don't listen to them
Do you realise what it means?

It affects the way you all work together
It affects everyone's KPIs
The support they give your customers
They may no longer want to try

Staff are no longer in the school yard
They shouldn't have to raise their hand
They're tired, stressed and overwhelmed
Do you really understand?

They might say their workload is extensive
Do you understand how much?
Are their limited tools or broken processes?
Is the pressure all too much?

Staff work so hard both day and night
Do you think it's good enough
If they feel gaslit and not respected?
Turning up to work would be so tough

Do your staff really feel supported?
Do you praise them as a team?
If their mental health is spiralling
Do you know what the end might mean?

## The workplace

The workplace can be so stressful
When deadlines and goals come first
We can easily forget our mental health
When we're so focused on our work

But it's important to remember
That our mental health's at risk
When we're not taking care of it
We simply can't perform at our best

Companies should create a safe environment
That openly talks about mental health
Offering their staff resources
To ensure they have some help

Talk to someone if you're struggling
Ask your doctor for advice
Use the tools the company offers you
So your mental health doesn't pay the price

We're all guilty of putting the workplace first
And not what's most important in our lives
But when life's cut short, what's the point?
Because all we've lost is time

## We're not family

Many companies say, 'We're family'
But that's not exactly true
Companies may want a family culture
But our family isn't you!

You might want a family dynamic
Of support and trust and care
A healthy relationship with colleagues
Although our family isn't there

Some families are dysfunctional
It's not always a happy affair
So when you refer to work as 'family'
Staff may not actually want to be there

We go home to our family
They're not the ones keeping us at work
Pressuring us to put up with behaviours
Or killing our self-worth

When companies say, 'We're family'
We feel pressure to accept
Mistreatment and poor boundaries
And putting our health at neglect

A family doesn't 'let you go'
When the times are tough
They help support and guide you
And they remind you 'you're enough'

So we might work together
Spending many hours naturally
We're colleagues, workmates and even friends
But we're not family

## *Life is hard enough*

We should be able to come to work each day
And work together as a team
Supporting one another
And following their dreams

We don't need a toxic workplace
Adding further stresses to our life
We all want peace and harmony
And we want a happy life

You never know somebody's story
You don't know what they've been through
Life throws us constant curveballs
Life can be difficult to do

We have a cost of living crisis
Staff are struggling with their mental health
Not all the household may be working
Some people are doing it all themselves

Staff may struggle with their physical health
They could live in constant pain
Ongoing pain is debilitating
Please don't put them through more strain

Why should we have to struggle in the workplace?
When there's bad behaviour from the top
Which can spread throughout the company
This behaviour needs to stop!

Why do people make it difficult?
Life can already be so tough
We don't need this constant chaos
Because life is hard enough!

# How do you expect us to be our best?

How do you expect us to be our best?
Within a toxic workplace
When we're all so very sleep deprived
From all the hours that we've faced

How do you expect us to be our best?
When we're constantly broken down
When we're blamed and disrespected
And this behaviour won't back down

How do you expect us to be our best?
When we've been made to feel so small
This culture constantly tears us down
With our backs against the wall

How do you expect us to be our best?
We're not working as a team
There's no respect and there's no trust
And there's constant gaslighting

How do you expect us to be our best?
When were blamed and have done no wrong
When we no longer want to raise our hand
It might be easier moving on

How do you expect us to be our best?
When we have no time for ourselves
Or quality time with friends and family
How can we focus on our health?

How do you expect us to be our best?
When we're torn so far down
We can't be our best for customers
If we always let them down

How do you expect us to be our best?
When we're all so burnt out
As we're constantly fighting fires
And having fears of doubt

How do you expect us to be our best?
There's no spring left in our step
There's no way staff can be their best
When they have nothing left

## Hey boss

I only had three hours sleep last night
But I finished that last minute request
You know, the one that was so urgent
I hope it was worth all my stress

I missed out on dinner with my kids last night
Once again the goal posts changed
Another presentation with no notice
I have to work while kids complain

I only sleep a few hours every night
As I constantly toss and turn
With the endless deadlines in my head
My health is becoming a concern

I heard you talking in the kitchen
About how you had such a great weekend
You saw your kids win sports games
And how you spent time with your friends

I wish I got to see my kids play sports
But once again I had no warning
You expected another last minute report
The one required for Monday morning

I spent my entire weekend working
To ensure I finished that report
Only to find out on Monday morning
That you had planned some time off work

I didn't need to work this weekend
I could have spent my time with family
This behaviour is so disrespectful
And it's so obvious to see

This week you called me every night
And again took up my personal time
My wife and I are struggling
And my marriage is in decline

I called you a couple of times this week
And I know that it was after hours
But it's funny how the tables turn
You don't answer my calls after hours

I finished that presentation
You know, when you were out to lunch
The one we should have worked on together
For that meeting that's so important

I'm tired of working unrealistic hours
And losing time with family
You have unrealistic expectations
And you always disagree

I'm missing special moments with my children
And I miss time with my wife
My kids are growing up before my eyes
And I'm missing out on life

You don't show good leadership
Or ensure we have balance of life and work
I don't get paid for these extra hours
And I'm so overworked

But hey boss, I'm glad you get time with family
And you clock off most days at five
Enjoying fun things every evening
And getting so much out of life!

## *A sinking ship*

Why do you think so many staff are leaving?
They're running for the door
They're tired of this behaviour
And they can't take it anymore

This business is in chaos
Can you even see what's going on
When you take a look around you
And see good people have all gone?

The ones left behind are so deflated
They're demoralised and unsure
They're dealing with the extra workload
Soon they'll be heading for the door

No-one's listening to the issues
No-one cares what's going on
Staff raise many things to management
But there's rarely a response

It's what happens with poor leadership
Staff lose respect and trust
When they have no faith in management
And their self-esteem is crushed!

Does this place have its own revolving door
Where employees constantly come and go
Giving a sense of instability
And leaving employees feeling low?

How is this not a warning sign?
When staff leave because of this
When staff have nothing left to give
The company is a sinking ship

## The revolving door

Today, I met a new staff member
They seemed to be real nice
We talked about our products
And they gave some great advice

We went through lots of training
And some customer visits too
They seemed to fit in perfectly
They'll be a great part of the crew

They haven't been here very long
But wait, they've just resigned
The revolving door takes another victim
As they leave this place behind

This revolving door keeps turning
As staff continually leave
It's the main warning sign of toxicity
And good results we won't achieve

This doesn't help our business grow
In fact it holds it back
Isn't it so obvious
This won't help us stay on track?

This door harms our reputation
And it takes up so much time
With endless ongoing recruitment
And retraining all the time

We wish this door would just stop turning
As another one bites the dust
Can you please just stop this damage
And be the company one can trust?

Please see the reason staff are leaving
The team can't take it anymore
It's so obvious to all of us
So, please stop this revolving door

## The promotion

If you promote employees in the workplace
The climb may be a little steep
Employees need to be supported
For them to take this leap

Leaders need to show that they believe in staff
And encourage them to climb
Offering them support and guidance
And offering them some time

Set up a plan to guide them
You need to help them learn and grow
It should be part of their development
You should want to see them grow

This is all part of leadership
And developing your team
Ensuring they have the opportunities
To be the best that they can be

You need to be their advocate
When they're not in the room
Make sure that you don't blame them
For things they didn't do

Do you help employees climb this ladder?
If not, you help them fall
Staff want to work towards promotions
With encouragement from all

## Why are toxic staff promoted?

Why are toxic staff promoted
If they haven't done their job
When there's many things outstanding
Or they're a continuous roadblock?

Are they good at playing the political game
Or how they manage up?
Do they tell you what you want to hear?
Are they a bully or corrupt?

How many staff go for promotions
But miss out on the role?
Even though they had the qualities
And experience for this role

When they have good reputations
And admiration from their teams
But then, the 'boys' club' wins again
As they hire from within

It's time to change the way for promotions
And look through another lens
At times management don't see what's going on
And they're the leader of their team

## Same shit, different day

Here we seem to go again
We face another day of abuse
Another day of constant yelling
Where we wonder what's the use

It's not a safe working environment
It's full of negativity and stress
We're constantly mistreated
No-one cares about our health

It's always unpredictable
It's constant chaos at every turn
We've never worked with such betrayal
Why do they never seem to learn?

I'm so tired of these constant games
That no staff wants to play
I have no other words to describe this
Except same shit, different day!

## *Worker burnout*

We have the weight upon our shoulders
With the pressure that we're under
The demands are just relentless
Like a storm with raging thunder

I drag myself to work each day
But I've been working half the night
My mind is cloudy, my body aches
And I'm losing strength to fight

This company just keeps pushing
And I'm giving them my all
But nothing seems to be enough
And they won't see me fall

Some days I give it all I have
But my all is only half the tank
This job takes all my energy
And without ever being thanked!

I don't have the energy to collaborate
And I know my mood can change
I feel I'm always irritable
As I go about my day

I have difficulty sleeping
It's hard to fall or stay asleep
I wake up with constant headaches
This endless pain is running deep

The constant stress from management
Seems to be passing down the line
They want so much productivity
And in such little time

My passion now has weakened
And I have lost my spark
I'm exhausted and depleted
From the intensity of work

How can leaders just not see
I'm battered and I'm bruised
And I'm just doing the best I can
But feel mentally abused?

Burnout is an epidemic
Employees around the globe all feel the same
It's spreading fast like wildfire
It's a fire we need to tame

Sometimes staff assist to burnout
We're our own worst enemy
We don't say 'no' to workloads
And we have this disease to please!

But even if we raise our hand
And highlight all the work we have to do
It doesn't seem to matter
Management still want us to follow through

We want to make a difference
And do right for the company
But we're not supported in our own health
And management just don't see

We need to work out our priorities
And put a stop to goalposts moving
Staff can't keep up with the workload
Nothing seems to be improving

Burnout can cause depression
And it affects your physical health
There's no energy for your family
Remember your health is wealth

Burnout can take so long to heal from
Many months or even years
Please make changes to your workplace
So all this pain can disappear

We need to stand up and use our voices
And end this worker burnout beast
We need to create a healthy balance
So employees don't find defeat

## *Leave means leave*

If your employee is on holidays
They need a break
They are entitled to a break
They are using their personal holiday time
This is their time
They may have saved up for months, or even years for a trip
It might be the only time they have
They might be spending time with family and friends
They haven't seen for years
Or someone who is ill
Don't expect them to work during this time
It's not fair
They are on holidays
Leave means leave

If your employee is sick
And requires time off
Don't pressure them into working
Don't ring them with questions
They need this time to recover
Message them asking, 'Is there anything you need?', or 'how can I help?'
Don't expect them to work during this time
It's not fair
They are sick
Leave means leave

If your employee is on carer's leave
They are caring for a loved one
Someone who may be very ill
Someone who may have limited time
They need this time with them, not to think about work

Message them asking, 'Is there anything you need?', or 'how can I help?'
Don't expect them to work during this time
It's not fair
Leave means leave

Create a culture where employees have the right to take time off when required and don't have to feel torn about work as well. Employees want a culture where they can enjoy their personal holidays without the burden of work, one that offers support when they are ill or caring for a loved one.

## *You're wrong!*

If you think being a leader
Is throwing your weight around
Or blaming one another
You're wrong!

If you think being a leader
Is bullying your team
Making them scared to speak up
You're wrong!

If you think being a leader
Is putting so much pressure on your team
As they work relentless hours
You're wrong!

If you think being a leader
Is gaslighting your team
And making them question their own ability
You're wrong!

If you think being a leader
Is micromanaging your team
Making them feel that they can't do their job
You're wrong!

If you think being a leader
Is constantly 'testing' your team
As you call them out in front of peers
You're wrong!

If you think staff don't see your behaviour
Or that you have their respect
If you think your team has trust in you
You're wrong!

You see, staff do see your behaviour
And they talk within the team
They're in tears and their exhausted
Causing frustration among the team

If you think you are a good leader
And staff are happy you're in charge
And they've put their faith and trust in you
You're wrong!

## When you look into the mirror

When you look into the mirror
What do you really see?
Do you actually see the leader
You aspired yourself to be?

Do you believe you've done your best
As the leader of your team
Giving staff a compelling vision
And sharing in their dreams?

Do you believe you have protected
All staff within your care?
Do you realise that's your job to do?
It's the reason you are there

Do you know leadership is an honour?
It has an impact on employees' lives
Have you done the best to care for them
Or have you put them through hard times?

Your staff all try to do their best
But they have their own lives too
They shouldn't have to use their personal time
Just trying to please you!

Do you show that you are vulnerable?
Do you show a human side?
Do you believe you are supportive
Or caused a rollercoaster ride?

When you look into this mirror
What changes will you guarantee?
Now, look deep into this mirror
What do you really see?

# *Can you see the forest for the trees?*

What does your company culture look like?
Have you found that common ground?
Is your team excited to come to work
When Monday morning comes around?

Companies have a responsibility
To provide a safe and healthy space
Please leave the egos at the door
And create a happy place

Does your team see you as a leader
Inspiring them to be their best
Giving a vision for the future
And recognising team success?

Do you set clear expectations
Or do the goal posts always move?
Do staff find it hard to please you
Because you always disapprove?

Are you too engrossed in other details?
Are you focusing on one thing?
Do you constantly blame each other?
What value do you bring?

Do you just focus on the top line
Or do you understand the weeds?
If you don't care about the issues
You're not likely to succeed

Have you caused some of these issues
Because you didn't listen to your team
And went against their judgement
Now the issues are extreme?

How do you help support your staff
When they raise their hands?
Do you actually hear what they are saying
Or do you just make more demands?

How have you contributed
When promoting staff within?
Do you help to guide and mentor them
Or just let them sink or swim?

Do you go and see your customers
And get insights first-hand?
To see what sales are up against
And really try to understand?

Do you trust your staff to do the job
You hired them to do?
Do you know when to apologise
Or give credit when it's due?

Do you have their backs when times are tough
Or do you throw them to the wolves?
Do you find a way to let others shine
Or just think about yourselves?

Do you truly know your leadership team
And how they treat the staff?
How they treat you and other leaders
Might be a very different path

Do you actually support mental health
Or just pretend you do?
Are you just ticking all the boxes
Or do you actually follow through?

Do you know if staff are suffering
With stress and anxiety
With constant worker burnout
Or inequality?

Do you have enough staff in each department
Or are you far too lean
Putting all that extra pressure
And extra hours on your team?

How much money has been wasted
Due to constant staffing needs?
The loss of knowledge and experience
And of company expertise?

Do you know what people talk about
Or the word upon the street?
What would they say about your company?
Would they want to join your team?

Do you realise not every manager
Should be responsible for a team?
They should not be managing people
Or there may be a toxic theme

Your staff are your biggest assets
Without them where would you be?
Success will always follow
With happy and valued employees

Can you really see the issues
In the team you thought you knew?
Can you see some of these issues
Might actually be you?

This one might be hard to answer
But it does need to be said
Are you the right person in the driver's seat
Or should you step aside instead?

Can you read yourself within this forest
Or will you just focus on the trees?
Do you have the self-awareness
To make the changes that you need?

It's all part of health and safety
And understanding all the risks
Promoting health and wellness
And ensure no bullying exists

Someone's life might be in crisis
They could be treading on thin ice
You could be triggering past emotions
And causing many sleepless nights

So, to all the 'leaders' out there
Please take a step back and see
What does your culture REALLY look like?
Can you see the forest for the trees?

## *Never get back that time*

Time is irreversible
It's one thing we can't get back
As it slips by so damn fast
And it's gone, just like that!

Time is our constant companion
It helps heal wounds and scars
We need to treasure every second
And live each day like it's our last

Staff shouldn't be working all these hours
It's not fair to the team
They should live life to the fullest
Not drowning for the company

So many staff work such long hours
Struggling with burnout and with stress
When they should be making memories
Not regretting time they didn't spend

When we leave our company
For whatever reason that might be
There's nothing extra for all those hours
They took from friends and family

Because of unrealistic workloads
And goalposts moving all the time
Staff have lost so many hours
And they'll never get back that time

## Why is it called 'human resources?'

Why is it called 'human resources?'
When humans are not a resource
We're not oil, coal or natural gas
But we are a powerful force

We're not a type of product
You can't just buy us off the shelf
We have feelings and emotions
And sometimes we need some help

'Human resources' feels impersonal
The human touch seems to be lost
It feels that we're not seen as a person
And the focus is not on us

## Human resources

HR forms part of 'leadership'
They're the gateway to the company
Developing and changing culture
And ensuring a positive theme

These are essential elements
Including pay and benefits
Recruiting, training and onboarding
And reinforcing values of the business

But it's said, HR don't look after staff
Their priority is the company
Staff are the company's biggest assets
Can you take more care of the team?

It's no good for the company
When staff constantly come and go
Losing expertise and knowledge
Won't help your company grow

Do you find it hard to recruit staff now?
Do you know why that might be?
What does your reputation look like?
What's talked about on the street?

Some HR staff may struggle
Because they do have empathy
They can see what's really going on
But they have to support the 'company'

The reality is staff are company
And they go hand in hand
Would you rather staff on stress leave
Or focus on business to expand?

What happens when staff are on stress leave?
How does that protect the company
When you're paying staff a salary
And there's a gap in productivity?

How do you support staff when they speak up?
Do you really listen to what they say?
Because all this helps your business grow
And affects your credibility

## The hiring process

Do you need to tighten your hiring process?
It's the first step into your company
But there's so many bad experiences
And some are so plain to see

Do you have a range of jobs that are advertised?
People can take hours to apply for a role
But then you gain some insider knowledge
And find out all jobs are on hold

This is a complete waste of time for candidates
And it's time they'll never get back
They're excited about possibilities
Then they find out there's no job to have

The ones who don't have the insider knowledge
Are left hanging without a reply
Because nobody communicates with them
And it was all a waste of their time

This certainly damages your branding
It's seen as a company candidates can't trust
Don't post roles that are not available
Or post roles so you're ticking a box

Why do we update and polish our resume'
Then load it up on the relevant portal
Just to duplicate all the work we've done
Why can't it automatically come full circle?

How many times do candidates apply for a role
Without even an automated reply
They don't know if someone received it
Was it even worth giving it their time?

Can you please streamline the interview process?
Sometimes it's just too steep
Can't you see the candidate can do the job
The first time that you meet?

Can you see that they are passionate
And excited to join your team?
You can't teach enthusiasm
But you risk losing them through time

Having to do so many interviews
Case studies and presentations
Takes so much time for everyone
And adds further frustrations

Why does the hiring process take so long?
Sometimes it takes months to achieve
And having to constantly follow up
Doesn't look good for your company

Another issue in the process
Is not hiring from within
Why compare to outside candidates
When there's staff capable to fit in?

Have faith in your internal candidates
Give them the space to learn and grow
Don't give outside candidates hope
Or waste their time when you say 'no'

Do candidates do psychological testing
Then get told they don't have the job
Because a particular skill is missing
But test results reveal the opposite?

Why bother with the testing
If you don't take results seriously?
It's a waste of time for candidates
And a waste of money for the company

How many times do candidates go for an interview
Only to be ghosted after the discussion?
They try to follow up with no response
And are made to feel that they're worth nothing

What about when candidates do presentations
That might take days to complete
And you want them to send you a copy
Now you have their knowledge if they find defeat?

They may not end up being right for the role
But make sure you let them know
Please offer constructive feedback
That will help them learn and grow

There's one thing that's ever so frustrating
When candidates have interviewed for a role
They're told the company's decided to 'reorganise'
And everything is now on hold!

Remember, behind every resumé and interview
Is a person with a family to feed
Is a person with bills that need paying
And this would be giving them anxiety

Can you imagine if each role they went for
All treated them in the same way?
All this would be so overwhelming
And make candidates struggle day to day

Remember you don't know their story
You don't know what's happening in their life
This process could be causing them so much pressure
And forcing their health to decline

They might not have current employment
And they're doing all they can
To find a company and an income
To meet their financial and personal demand

This is so very demoralising
It affects your candidates' mental health
It affects your company branding
And won't help your branding excel

So let's get better at the hiring process
And remember the human being
It's so much more than just a process
And a key introduction to your company!

### *When employees leave*

Leaving a toxic work environment
Is the smartest thing employees do
They may not want to leave the company
But in fact, they're leaving you!

Employees are leaving *poor leadership*
Or maybe no leadership at all
They might be leaving a *blaming culture*
Because they'll no longer take the fall

They're taking back their power
And setting their own boundaries
They're protecting their integrity
As this workplace is now history

It's too late to try and save them
When they have already resigned
You can't appreciate them as they're leaving
If you didn't in their time

There may be no training or development
Employees might be set up to fail
Employees want career progression
With the growth that would entail

Leaders think employees are the ones who lose
They say it is 'their loss'
We'll just find someone to replace them
As they increase another cost

Leaders may think it's an easy process
And new employees they'll just appoint
But if they can't see why staff are leaving
I think they've missed the point!

Leaders may think it's an opportunity
To employ more qualified staff
But when your reputation's 'toxic'
It cuts good candidates in half

Top candidates want to work with innovation
They want a company they can trust
They want to be respected
And get on with doing what they love

Leaders think staff are the ones who lost
But that's so far from the truth
Employees are standing up for themselves
And their mental health

Employees are better off without this company
If they can now actually sleep at night
As they stop dealing with toxicity
They can doze 'til morning light

The *company* is the one who suffers
When customers lose respect
Dealing with this constant turbulence
They can see the disconnect

The *company* is the one who suffers
As employees continually come and go
Taking all that knowledge with them
Doesn't allow the company growth

The *company* is the one who suffers
As they start recruitment once again
With time spent finding other candidates
And retraining once again

The *company* is the one who suffers
Because the budget is now lost
As more money's wasted on recruitment
With another rising cost

The *company* is the one who suffers
As their name comes into play
When ex-employees tell their story
Of why they left this company

When employees leave your company
What's your separation process?
Do you spend time with staff to understand
The reasons for their exit?

This shouldn't be a three line survey
It should be a proper conversation
So management can understand
How to improve the situation

Employees worked hard for your company
So acknowledge the time they served
Make sure you understand their leaving
And show the respect that they deserve

How do you use this information
To make it part of staff retention?
Do you readdress the issues
That lead to resignations?

When employees constantly leave your company
*Alarm bells* should be ringing
There's red flags within your culture
And your business won't be winning

If your company is losing 25% of staff or higher in one year, that is a major red flag and indicates underlying problems in the workplace. If you have a high staff turnover, how can you not see the signs that there is a serious issue?

People mainly leave for the following reasons:

- Toxic work environment
- Poor leadership
- Poor management
- Overworked and burnt out
- Low salaries
- No development opportunity
- Lack of appreciation

A high turnover of staff has a significant negative impact on your business and your bottom line. With a constant turnover of staff, how does that help your company grow? How can you not see the signs when it causes the following issues?

- Time wasted going through the recruitment process again
- Increased recruitment costs
- Knowledge and expertise walk out the door
- Time wasted on constant retraining
- Increased workload for other employees
- Decreased morale
- Damage to customer relationships
- Damage to brand and reputation
- Damage to your position in the market

## Exclusion in the workplace

When staff feel excluded in the workplace
It impacts in negative ways
Decreases morale and productivity
And ensures the staff hard days

Exclusion can come for different reasons
Such as gender or disability
It can be age or sexual orientation
Or an employee's ethnicity

Exclusion has a negative impact
On the wellbeing of employees
It creates a toxic workplace
Where staff don't feel at ease

Staff can be left out of social gatherings
Be ignored or ostracised
They can be treated with such disrespect
It makes them feel demoralised

They can be denied advancement
Which doesn't help with their career
Sometimes they're micromanaged
As their manager interferes

Exclusion makes employees feel unwelcome
They can feel uncomfortable at work
They can be constantly criticised
And be harrassed while they're at work

Don't allow staff to feel excluded
Ensure inclusion and diversity
Have zero tolerance for bullying
And create a safe place for staff to be

## Your customers' experience

At the end of bad behaviour
And who looks on as a witness
It is in fact your customers
The ones who take care of your business

What is this doing to your customers?
They can tell when something's wrong
They can see that staff are suffering
If they don't stay there very long

Have you done the best thing for your customers
With decisions that you've made?
Have your customers been impacted
By the leadership you've displayed?

Customers can tell staff don't have passion
Or that they're just ticking a box
They can see the bad decisions made
They can see when hope is lost

Customers might have the same reaction
To some leaders in the team
Not wanting to deal with them at all
It doesn't make a winning team!

When you choose to be a leader
Please don't be oblivious
We're here to serve our customers
So think of their experience

## Let's get serious about the workload

Let's get serious about the workload
It's got so far out of hand
Employees are working unrealistic hours
When will management understand?

The current workload is not sustainable
Staff are overworked and underpaid
They're rewarded with more work to do
And it's how mistakes are made

This causes stress and burnout
There's reduced productivity
Some of this may be reactive
And causes negativity

When staff have so much of a workload
There's no time for innovation
There's a lack of creativity
Which can cause so much frustration

There's clearly a lack of understanding
Of how much employees actually do
Fuelled with constant new requests
As staff are asked for more to do

There's impractical expectations
When we're requested to do a task
With an unrealisitic deadline
Because you don't know what you've asked

You don't realise that task you asked for
Takes about four days to compile
But you want it presented by tomorrow
How can that data be worthwhile?

The workload may not be aligned
To the skills and interests of the staff
Leading to job unfulfillment
As it takes much longer to do the task

Some staff have a bigger workload
Or may not be trained properly in their role
Which can make work much more challenging
Leading to a decreased morale

## *Re-evaluate your workplace*

For employees in a toxic workplace
Remember, it can make you sick
We've all accepted bad behaviour
Putting our mental health at risk

You may try to calm situations
Or think that things will change
Feeling helpless in the workplace
Won't be positive to your day

Are you feeling disconnected
Or that you don't belong?
You might feel that it's just all too much
But you need to stay so strong

Are you feeling you don't matter
Or that your voice isn't heard?
Do you feel there's no development?
Has your career path been deferred?

If you won't put up with bad behaviour
In a relationship or at home
Why accept it in the workplace?
It's not something we should condone

Just don't lose sight of who you are
Or get lost in a toxic crowd
Because once you lose that person
You need to fight so hard

Sometimes we can weaken
Thinking life's too hard to take
But let's focus on the positives
For changes we need to make

Sometimes you need to feel that all is lost
Before you can find yourself
You'll find the strength to come back fighting
For your physical and mental health

You train your mind to be so strong
And keep emotions in better check
Learning to react to your emotions
Will help you be your best

But when you look deep inside yourself
And find your inner strength
You'll see behaviour that's not acceptable
For your own mental health

You'll want to take your power back
You'll want a company to embrace
For you to make the right decision
Re-evaluate your workplace

## *When staff want a pay rise*

Why don't you take me seriously
When I ask you for a raise?
I work hard for this company
As I go about my day

I work so many extra hours
And I deliver what you ask
I have so many years experience
You know I can do this task

If I ask you for a pay rise
I feel it's well-deserved
Because of my dedication to this company
Which I know you have observed

It's not comfortable to ask for a pay rise
But it's getting hard to make ends meet
So I'm asking for a reason
I have a family I need to feed

But if you say 'no' to a pay rise
You'll make me feel that I'm not valued
I might have to leave this company
And find one where I am valued

So think about your expectations
And how much work is actually in this role
It can be completely overwhelming
And this job can take its toll

It will cost you more in resources
As you start recruitment once again
Taking time for all those interviews
Hoping new staff will just fit in

It takes months for full induction
Training and getting up to speed
Hoping they don't leave you
After a short time in the company

It will cost you more to replace me
Than if you just paid me what I'm worth
So please value your employees
And please pay what they deserve

## *Open door policy*

Do you highlight an open door policy?
How many staff actually walk through?
Staff want open communication
But they might be scared to talk to you

Do you come across as caring?
Or do you show empathy?
Staff worry about the fall out
And what the pain might be

There might be issues in the workplace
You might not like what they say
You might not take them seriously
And they have to work there every day

It takes guts to come and talk to you
And if you just brush it off
You'll make them feel so under valued
And that they are not enough

It's a big step for staff to walk through your door
Clearly something needs to change
So, listen carefully to what they tell you
And help make this a better place

Your staff are giving you the chance
To highlight their concerns
Giving you first hand ability
To understand and learn

To learn how this issue might affect your staff
Your business and your brand
It might contribute to losing customers
So make sure you understand

If you don't really hear this conversation
Or don't action issues raised
You lose your employee's respect and trust
It's not the way you should behave

Your reputation is at stake here
And the next steps that you take
Will you action this appropriately
Or will you make a big mistake?

## Don't shoot the messenger

Staff are scared to speak up in the workplace
Fearing retaliation or revenge
They may even think they will be fired
And they would have to start again

They might be seen to be a troublemaker
Or that they just want to complain
It might harm someone's reputation
Making it hard for others to refrain

Staff may think their concerns will be ignored
And be discouraged with no change
Wondering why they even bothered
And face the same issues once again

Staff may fear they will be ostracised
And have no support from peers
It would make it hard to do their job
As they continue to work in fear

It's important to speak up in the workplace
Although it's extremely difficult
You need to speak up to make the changes
Or they'll be no difference

Staff should be able to speak up in the workplace
Without fear of retribution
It's not something staff do lightly
They just want a resolution

There's a reason staff take this risk
Something seriously needs to change
Leaders have a workplace responsibility
To protect everyone in the team!

Leaders should take the conversation seriously
They should then investigate
And give employees a resolution
They should not discriminate

Leaders should also give employees skills
To identify bullying behaviour
Enforce anti-bullying policies
And ensure a stop to this behaviour!

Staff are tired of these environments
And just want to protect their peers
The constant negative conversations
And to stop the tears and fears

Some feel they have nothing left to lose
They're not afraid to lose their job
They're already treated poorly
And know this behaviour will not stop!

The ones who make things hard when staff speak up
Are definitely imposter leaders
Because these are destructive actions
That don't come from any 'true leader'

Others are inspired by colleagues for speaking up
And for choosing to take the risk
Fighting for a safe work environment
And ensuring the workplace is positive

Ensure it's safe to speak up in the workplace
So this behaviour's not repeated
If staff don't feel it's safe to do
You've failed them as their leader

Remember the one who speaks up is not the problem
And they should not be victimised
They're the ones who are trying to help you
So ensure you don't pick a side

When employees speak up in the workplace
This information you need to register
Raising toxic behaviour is a cry for help
So please don't shoot the messenger!

## *Is your leadership team scared of you?*

Many leaders are uncomfortable speaking up
To the highest leader in their team
Because if you don't know the answer
They reply back with a scream

This is not just about raising issues
This can be for business day to day
But if they don't feel they can question you
Their confidence starts to fade

If you're not allowed to question
How do you make informed decisions?
How can you figure out a better way
If you don't allow the questions?

It's hard when you give a direction
And the team doesn't agree with you
But they're not allowed to question
And they just have to follow through

How can you have deep discussions?
It's what any company should want
You should not be made to feel stupid
Because you don't have the right response

Nobody has all the answers
We have different knowledge within the team
You should want an open dialogue
And work together as a team

If your leadership team can't talk to you
Because you don't make them feel at ease
And if your leadership team is scared of you
You've failed them and your employees!

## It's time

It's time to speak up in the workplace
It's time to say, 'No more!'
It's time to take our power back
And stop giving bullies 'the floor'

It's time to cut out their behaviour
And put them in their place
It's time to call each one out
As it's such a disgrace!

Bullying is not okay
In any type of form
We need to all stand up together
And stop bullying from being 'the norm'

If we stay silent in the workplace
We give the bully complete control
So let's all create a united front
And have everyone enrolled

Let's make it safe to use our voices
Because this abuse is not okay
Encourage each other to use their voice
And stop abuse happening every day!

I'm asking for employees to have the courage
To take the front of the line
For workplaces to become 'united'
So everyone knows 'It's time!'

## *How to speak up in the workplace*

Most employees don't speak up in the workplace due to the fear of repercussions. It's a very tough and brave thing to do. Sometimes things are happening in the organisation that the leader may not be aware of, and there needs to be change. As the 'leader', this actually gives them the opportunity to do something about it. That's one of main reasons people feel they need to speak up; they just want a change to current behaviour. And this is not something the employee does lightly. A lot of thought, and sometimes anxiety, goes into their decision to do this in the first place. This is due to what they want to raise and the potential repercussions they will endure following the conversation.

I have spoken up in the workplace and had a 'courageous conversation'. It was the hardest thing I've ever had to do at work. I thought I could just resign and make it someone else's problem, or I could try to make a positive change for myself and my colleagues. I chose to try and make a change because I didn't actually want to leave. So, if you have the courage to have this conversation, be prepared. This is what I did.

Request a meeting with the highest leader

1. Be prepared. You can't just come in and randomly talk about the problems or people. You need to have a structure.
2. What is the problem? Have examples for each scenario you want to discuss.
3. What does this mean for the business, the brand, the team, the customers?
4. How has it affected the above?
5. Did it cost the company extra money?
6. Did it lead to the loss of a contract or customer?
7. What was/is the ripple effect?

8. How often has it happened?
9. What is your solution?

There may also be examples that you won't have a solution for, especially if its around specific behaviour. These need to be discussed carefully, but again, have clear examples, so the leader can understand the issues and investigate the situation.

Ensure the leader understands what you are raising with them and why. Ask them what actions they will take and what the next step will be. Ask for a follow-up conversation within a few weeks to check the progress and potential outcomes. If nobody speaks up, nothing will change and the issues will continue and more than likely, worsen over time.

**You may be targeted**

You may feel you'll be exposed after speaking up. Too often employees are targeted for speaking up in the workplace. Targeting is when people may treat you differently. 'Leaders' may completely ignore you, or you may be ignored in meetings or events. You might be blamed for something or be given a hard time by other 'leaders' or employees. You might be seen as a troublemaker. At times, this can be pretty obvious behaviour. Ensure you document each scenario, as you may be covered from a legal perspective. Please seek your own legal due diligence here. And you may also want to do so before before speaking up.

Many countries have laws with regard to whistleblowing. So again, seek your own due diligence for legal advice in your country as they will differ.

As a leader, you should want to know what's happening in your business, so ensure a safe system where employees can speak up regardless of what it is - and without becoming a target. Remember, it's really hard for employees to speak up and they are speaking up because something is wrong in your business. Whatever the reason is for speaking up, employees are giving 'leaders' a chance to address the issues and make positive change.

If a 'leader' doesn't take your conversation seriously, you will be very disappointed and feel unvalued. You are speaking up for a reason. But remember, you may be raising the fact that there is toxicity in the workplace, which is on their watch. That's not a good scenario for them to be in. But if they don't take your conversation seriously, that's a major red flag in itself and it's time to get out and find a company that will not only appreciate you, but one where the culture is built on safety. And if you're wondering what my outcome was after speaking up—I resigned from the company!

If you're struggling with any aspect of your work environment, consider contacting your doctor or a therapist for guidance. There are many resources available, such as hotlines, support groups and mental health professionals, that can provide support and guidance.

## *Please don't suggest to stay*

If a friend is struggling in a toxic workplace
Please don't suggest they stay there and keep their head down
And just get on with their job
Workplace trauma is very real
It can take a very long time to heal, and there may be ongoing triggers

You are telling them to continue accepting unacceptable behaviour
that is already taking its toll on them and their health
Companies have different levels of toxicity
And while none of it is right, you do learn to deal with some of it
Many of us have, but we all have our breaking point!
We can only take it for so long and none of it is acceptable

However, when it's so bad that it's affecting your mental health,
your personal health, your ability to sleep, your personal time,
and your relationships, it's definitely not a good place to be.
When you're thinking, 'It's easier to just not be here'
You need to get out—fast!

If your friend was in a toxic and abusive relationship, you
wouldn't want them to stay in it
You would want them to get out of it
You might even help them to get out of it
Sometimes, the workplace is the toxic relationship

The workplace should NOT make people sick!

If you love the company you work for because it has a great
culture, and everyone treats each other with kindness and
respect, and works as a team, you are lucky to have found it.

### *We learned what not to do*

When we're in a toxic workplace
With so many examples as discussed
Sometimes we wonder what we learned there
Because the focus wasn't us

Our career path may be halted
We didn't get the chance to learn and grow
As we had to deal with bad behaviour
That constantly took its toll

There was no training or development
And when we think it through
We feel our time at this company was wasted
But we actually learned what not to do!

## *What if?*

What if your industry is healthcare?
Staff deal with patients' lives each day
But if they endure this endless bullying
It may compromise patient safety

What if your industry is manufacturing?
And leaders won't listen to their team
Of safety issues they keep raising
Can you see the risk this means?

What if your industry is construction?
It already has its risks
But if you add toxic behaviour
It could cause workplace death!

What if your industry is mining?
There's already dangerous situations
Like cave ins, floods and rockfalls
Please don't add mental health complications

What if your industry is male dominated
And women aren't treated with respect?
They've earned their seat at the table just like you
And shouldn't be treated with neglect

Due to abuse and pressure staff are under
Gruelling shifts and lack of breaks
Employees safety could be compromised
Can you really see here what's at stake?

## *What does the future look like?*

What does the future look like
For one who's been so traumatised?
As they had to deal with a toxic culture
Of bullying and being criticised

They also saw their colleagues suffer
And work so much overtime
They've seen tears and fears and heartache
They've seen their colleagues' health decline

Sometimes staff have had to make the hard decision
To resign from a job they love
'Cause the behaviour's been so disrespectful
And their mental health is shot!

Many staff have given you all they have to give
They worked long hours and weekends too
But why did you treat them so poorly
When they worked so hard for you?

So now they find a new employer
Where they have to start anew
Hoping their mental health will stop declining
But it's not what they should have had to do

They shouldn't have been put in a position
Where they always felt under attack
Because you didn't offer a safe workplace
So they had to take their power back

If only they were treated kindly
And were treated with respect
They'd still be working for your company
With no poor health effect

But how do they move forward now?
When they still feel they cannot trust
When they've lost their spark and confidence
And now therapy is a must

Employees are scared to join another workplace
As they fear the same behaviour
Which will set them further backwards
And once again put their health in danger

It takes time to heal from this adversity
Some will never be the same
You don't see what you do to your employees
When you play this bullying game

## We'll fight for what is right

Let's all stand up to the bullies
And try to make a change
To create a safe and happy workplace
And have all the team engaged

Let's all call out bad behaviour
The ones who gaslight, blame and shame
You don't see what you initiate
We'll no longer play this game

Let's all try to make a difference
And make this a better place
As we protect our colleagues
And ensure that they are safe

Your behaviour can be deadly
So we'll fight with all our might
We'll no longer be at your mercy
And we'll fight for what is right!

Let's *all* enforce a *zero tolerance*
And make the workplace safe and sound
Stop the ripple effect of bullying
So it's a healthy place to be around

## STOP the bullying!

This is a plea to stop the bullying
And make the workplace safe
Can we say, **'NO MORE!'** to bullying
And create a psychologically safe workplace?

We've all had enough of bullying
These victims are your employees
So I'm speaking up on their behalf
Let's put an end to this disease

I ask that you put a stop to bullying
And make your own pledge to this cause
Because people who are suffering
Could be family who are yours!

They may already have some struggles
And their workplace increases pain
It might make them question living
Because they're so tired from all the strain

So let's stand united all around the globe
Pledging to do whatever it takes
To banish workplace bullying universally
And make a psychologically safe workplace

## You don't see the broken human being

At the end of all this bullying
Is a broken human being
They've been battered and they've been bruised
Because they had to face this adversity

They chose to join your company
With what you sold them in your interview
But you failed this human being
Because your company didn't follow through

This was not what they agreed to
As they came to work each day
They agreed to pay and benefits
Not needing therapy along the way

They may now struggle trusting others
Or they may have PTSD
They may have depression or anxiety
They're broken in ways you'll never see

They may have already dealt with trauma
Or illness in the family
Life may already have been so difficult
And you just ensured more grief

It can take years to heal from adversity
Or the pain might stay for life
But as you just go about your day
You don't see what's left behind

You don't see the broken person
Trying to pick up the pieces unforeseen
Please assess your own behaviour
Because you don't see the broken human being

## *Before suicide takes another life*

Let me make myself very clear
Everyone in the workplace is a human being
Who all have feelings and emotions
Bullying affects leaders and employees

Let me remind you of some outcomes
Insomnia and isolation
Depression, anxiety, PTSD
Are all unbearable situations

All this is workplace trauma
And it's killing employees
These are your colleagues and your team mates
And this practice needs to cease!

*We MUST STOP bullying in the workplace*
*Employees have paid the ultimate price*
*Wake up and pay attention*
*Before suicide takes another life!*

When you're in a position of power,
make sure you don't use it to ruin someone's life!

*Jo Woodhouse*

I was deeply touched by a song I recently heard about bullying, and one that will resonate with people from all over the globe for different reasons.

I invite you to take a moment, download and immerse yourself in the powerful lyrics of **Eva Campbell's song, 'People'**.

Let its melody transport you to a realm of empathy and understanding, where the shared human experience shines through.

Eva writes:

> I wrote 'People' during lockdown, when I was spending a lot of time reflecting on my life, what's important to me and what message I wanted to share through my music.
>
> All through my life I stuck out like a sore thumb. I always wore what I wanted and am a bit of a proud nerd - hence the "reading books and wearing funky kicks" lyric! I wasn't 'unpopular' per se - but I seemed to have a target on my back. I think because I never shied away from being myself, even when people didn't like it.
>
> In my childhood I was picked on, but it was only in my teenage years I realised the effects bullying was having on me, and that's what has stuck with me to this day. One example of it is, I would go to parties and a gang of guys my age and older would throw food and drinks over me and taunt me - something no fifteen year old girl ever wants to experience. The same people can't even look me in the eye anymore, which I suppose is a good thing, because I hope they didn't and won't ever do it to anyone else.

*What upset me the most and still does to this day are the people - my 'friends' - never stuck up for me, or told these people to stop. Maybe if they hadn't been afraid to confront the people who were doing this to me, it wouldn't have happened so much and the bullies would have had a wakeup call.*

*Now, I will always advocate for the importance of not being a bystander, which I hope I've conveyed through the emotion of the song.*

*If you see anyone suffering, or anyone being mistreated - speak up. It could be life-changing for someone.*

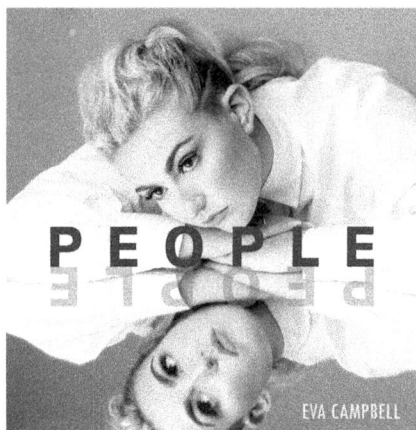

The lotus flower emerges from muddy waters to bloom beautifully, symbolising enlightenment, spiritual growth and overcoming negativity. As it is very personal to me, I have this symbol as a tattoo.

In this scenario, muddy waters represent a toxic and negative culture, while a beautiful bloom symbolises the potential for growth, resilience and transformation.

There is always hope and opportunity to overcome a toxic and bullying culture and transform it into a kind, caring, supportive, inclusive, and psychologically safe culture for everyone.

# BUILDING A POSITIVE WORK ENVIRONMENT

By changing behaviours, you can help create a workplace culture that is caring and supportive of mental health, and a more positive experience for your employees. Your company culture must be lived and breathed from the top; however, it also needs to be made clear that employee wellbeing is everyone's responsibility. Here are some ways to make positive change in your company and build a solid foundation.

- **Create a people first culture:** Leadership is about your employees, so create a culture where you put your employee first. This will reduce staff turnover, increase productivity, enhance company brand, improve customer service, and boost innovation and creativity.

- **Create your CORE values:** These are fundamental beliefs and principles that guide your company culture and behaviour. They allow employees to strive for a common goal. Decide what's most important to your company, your customers and your community. Ensure they are led from the top and they are embedded into all aspects of the company culture.

- **Lead by example:** Staff are more likely to take mental health seriously when leaders do the same. Set a good example by talking about your own mental health, getting help when required, and setting work/life boundaries. Ensure you allow your team to do the same. It will backfire if you are taking mental health seriously but expecting your team to work long hours and on weekends.

- **Create a culture of trust:** All staff want a company they can trust. Make sure you follow through on all you offer them or what you sold them in the interview process. Create a safe space for them to be able to speak up or discuss any personal scenarios they may need support with.

- **Create a culture of morale and unity:**  All staff should be able to speak up and voice their issues, concerns and challenges in a safe space. They should be able to call out unethical behaviour without the risk of retaliation or being targeted. If employees don't feel safe to speak up, issues will continue to fester and grow and will only get worse over time.

- **Create a culture of respect:** All staff come to work for a reason. They want to be a respected member of the team for the work they do. Create a culture where everyone is treated with kindness and consideration regardless of their background.

- **Create a culture of caring:** Staff want a culture where they can enjoy their personal holidays, and one that offers support when they are ill or caring for a loved one, without the burden of work.

- **Create a culture of protection:** Protect staff from bullying, harassment and discrimination.  Ensure ALL staff know that a toxic environment will not be tolerated and ensure it is a safe space for people to speak up without retribution.

- **Create a culture of growth and one to learn from:** Instead of blaming employees for making  mistakes, focus on learning from them. We all make mistakes, it's part of life. This will help create a culture where employees are not afraid to make mistakes and where they are encouraged to take risks.

- **Create a results driven culture:** Allow employees to work to their own timetables, where possible, around families, wellbeing and personal situations. If the company is getting results, do staff really need to work 8.30 am - 5.00 pm? Do they really need to be in the office? Look at all that wasted time sitting in traffic? If not all roles can do this, align the ones who can't via other benefits.

- **Offer training programs and create a safe culture:** Provide programs on 'leadership and development', 'mental health in the workplace' and 'mental health first aid.' Ensure ongoing training programs for your leaders. Organise mental health speakers to run sessions for your team. Create policies against toxic behaviours and provide training to employees on how to recognise and respond to them. Ensure proper training for all employees when they progress or are promoted to a new role, especially if they are responsible for people for the first time. Ensure ongoing training for all people leaders.
    o **Induction:** Ensure a proper induction program for all new employees with a training and development roadmap. Don't expect employees to get things right if you haven't trained them. Every employee, including leadership, requires ongoing learning and development.

- **Provide resources:** Ensure employees have access to resources to improve their mental health, such as employee assistance programs (EAP), online resources and mental health apps. Ensure employees also know where to find these resources.

- **Promote self-care:** Encourage employees to take care of their mental health by practicing self-care activities, such as exercise, meditation and spending time with family and friends. This also includes understanding the current workload and expectations of your staff.

- **Promote teamwork and collaboration:** Encourage employees to work together and collaborate on projects. This will create a more supportive work environment and build trust within the team.

- **Celebrate the successes:** When employees achieve success, make sure to celebrate their accomplishments, regardless of how large or small. This will boost morale and create a more positive work environment where staff feel appreciated.

- **Recognize and reward good work:** When employees do a good job, be sure to recognise and reward them. This will show them their hard work is appreciated and they are valued members of the team. You may have a yearly award program, but ensure you have something on a monthly or regular basis to help motivate staff along the way.

- **Create an open culture:** Encourage staff to talk about their mental health and to seek help if they need it. Promote a supportive work environment.

- **Offer flexible work arrangements:** Flexible work arrangements can help employees reduce stress as they try to balance their work and personal lives. This could include hybrid roles or flexitime. Remember also, COVID has changed people and some people may no longer work well in a busy office.

- **Systems and tools:** Systems and tools play a crucial role in enhancing productivity and employee satisfaction. It is so frustrating to waste time due to poor technology, so ensure you have the right tools, processes and technology in place for your team to be efficient and able to perform their jobs efficiently and successfully.

Building a company culture does not happen overnight. It takes time and lots of effort from everyone to build a caring, supportive and positive culture. However, the investment in creating a positive culture is definitely worth it, leading to substantial benefits for both employees and the company.

## How to embed a culture into your company

It's critical to build a company culture. A company culture is individual to each company. But how do you embed it into your company? You need to ensure ALL employees live and breathe it. The highest leader must lead by example. Senior leaders need to be authentic about the culture and lead by example, or the staff will know it's not real. Remember, employees will follow the leader!

**Work out what your CORE values will be. Decide what's most important to:**
- your company
- your customers
- your community

**What do you want your company and your employees to stand for?**
- How will you live and breathe it every day?
- How will you be reminded of it?
- How does it resonate with the team?
- If employees are not following it, how will staff be reminded of it?

**Hire the right people for your culture:**
- Ensure new employees align with your company's CORE values.
- What are specific skills or experience—are they engaged and productive?
- Ask specific questions that can bring through your CORE values in the response.
- Ensure new employees understand the culture they are coming into.

**Induction:**
Through a 'new employee induction process', ensure that understanding of the company culture is part of the program and what is expected of the employee. Also know how to address it when employees or leaders aren't following it.

**Ongoing reminders:**
Your company CORE values need to become your company philosophy. They need to be at the 'top of mind' for employees. It can't be assumed that everyone knows and follows them. It requires constant reminding.

**Ways to do this regularly are:**
- Commence leadership meetings with a reminder of CORE values
- Launch, relaunch or remind of CORE values in training sessions
- Ensure ongoing training sessions
- Commence monthly meetings with a reminder of CORE values
- Incorporate in newsletters
- Emails and email signatures
- Monthly lunch and learns – talk about one CORE value each meeting, highlight good examples and/or have employees present a scenario where they 'lead by example'
- Screensavers
- Create CORE value champions

**Incorporate the CORE values into the company so employees can see that you take them very seriously. You can do this through:**
- The hiring process
- Performance discussions
- Business discussions – how are the CORE values being used to guide actions and outcomes?

**Recognise and reward employees:**

Recognise employees who are living, breathing and leading by example, the company CORE values. This also sends a positive message to other employees that they are appreciated for what they are doing. This may lead to other employees also following their lead.

**Review your culture:**

A new culture needs time to grow so have a yearly review, where the leadership team can check and adjust. Utilise employee engagement surveys. But don't just tick the box of doing the survey—you need to action the results. What's the point of doing a survey if you do nothing about the results?

## *A good company culture*

A good company culture should feel like a warm embrace
Staff should feel safe and secure
They should have support when in the workplace
Or when they have personal issues to endure

A good company culture has supportive leaders
Who show kindness and respect
Don't tolerate toxic behaviour
Or office politics

A good company culture is collaborative
Showing the way when you are lost
Helping you reach your full potential
And not doing business at any cost

A good company culture is supportive
Making you feel like you belong
It gives you hope when you're feeling down
And helps you to be strong

A good company culture is inclusive
And welcomes new employees
Regardless of their backgrounds
They should put everyone at ease

A good company culture is fair and equitable
Staff are rewarded for their work
They set clear expectations
And ensure staff aren't overworked

A good company culture is conversations
Giving staff the chance to learn and grow
They are challenged to be the best they can
And to reach their full potential

A good company culture is transparent
With management communications to the staff
On key decisions and the future
Not giving information by the half

A good company culture works together
And is productive as a team
Ensuring staff are motivated
With a happy and healthy theme

A good company culture is rewarding
Where staff can see the work they do
Is really making a difference
And the company actually follows through

A good company culture has fun and laughter
And everyone understands their roles
As the team works towards a purpose
And achieving company goals

## *Let's create the best work culture*

Let's create the best work culture
With candidates knocking down our door
Wanting to come and work with us
Because we're challenged and empowered

They want to join our company
Because the word upon the street
Is that we can trust each other
And we're valued as a team

They know we all show respect
And we hear each other out
We mentor and promote our staff
We know what our vision is about

We know career progression
Will keep our team wanting to stay
It's a major factor to retention
As staff have satisfaction day to day

We offer great benefits at this company
We make sure we pay staff well
We offer training and development
So we help our staff excel

But it's more than just the benefits
It's because we actually care
About fostering a culture
That supports wellbeing and mental health

Employees are appreciated
For all the work they do
We know constant recognition
Will motivate both me and you

We try and keep a work/life balance
And ensure no-one's overworked
We adhere to what we promised you
Through your interview process

We have a great company culture
Because we have a leadership that cares
They've made a safe working environment
That will grow and flourish through the years

## *Psychological safety in the workplace*

Psychological safety in the workplace
Is a shared belief that it is safe
To share ideas and ask the questions
And where staff can admit to a mistake

There's no fear of repercussions
Staff can be vulnerable without distress
It is such a crucial element
Of a healthy and productive workplace

When leaders care about psychological safety
Employees feel comfortable sharing ideas
They can share their viewpoints openly
Without having any fears

Our leaders will check how they can help you
Confirm what your development plan should be
Ask how they can do better as your leader
So you realise what you want to achieve

This creates an environment where staff feel valued
And respected as part of the team
It leads to increased job satisfaction
And it increases productivity

It's about ensuring safety in the workplace
And prioritising staff self-care
Allowing employees to be themselves
In any way they share

It's about creating a safe place for everyone
Leaders, managers and employees
Because every staff member here has feelings
And we care about our entire team

Our leaders will embrace psychological safety
And they will play a pivotal role
They will implement safe working practices
And ensure a safe workplace for all

## *Lead with heart*

Lead with heart means to be authentic
Inspiring and compassionate
It means you put your people first
Creating a caring work environment

Leaders aren't afraid to show they're vulnerable
Or for sharing their own experience
Showing their emotions to employees
Shouldn't be seen as a weakness

Leaders care about their employees
And for the wellbeing of their teams
They are always understanding
Allowing employees to be themselves

Leaders set the tone for their workplace culture
They're authentic and show empathy
They lead by their own example
And inspire other employees in their team

They create a sense of community
Celebrate the wins along the way
They show support and stimulation
As staff go about their day

Leaders celebrate diversity
Creating a safe space within the team
Where staff feel included and respected
And everyone's valued in the team

Leaders have a clear vision of the future
They give their team autonomy
They are hopeful and optimistic
And believe in their employees

## Leadership

A leader should have a vision
They should create a happy team
They should be leading by example
With excitement and empathy

A leader is not just anyone
They're one we actually want to follow
They build a strong work culture
And give us vision for tomorrow

Leadership should be a holistic approach
Every manager has a part to play
Bringing all the teams together
For the wellbeing of the company

This team sets the standards for the company
And that everybody's looking up to
They should be leading by example
Ensuring employees that they follow through

They set clear expectations
And help keep everyone on track
They support with any issues
And they have each other's back

They have a responsibility
To protect and guide their team
And in return their staff will thrive
As they build their self-esteem

They help empower others
And work with integrity
They thank staff for all their efforts
And have the right priorities

They show that they are vulnerable
As they connect with others in their team
They can see their team's potential
And help fulfil their dreams

They celebrate successes
And support when things go wrong
They gain respect and trust from others
Where all staff can get along

They support staff when they raise their hand
And offer them advice
Checking in on the progression
And stepping in when things aren't right

They remember staff all deal with
Many things within their life
They ensure a healthy balance
And help out when they're in strife

And remember, anyone can be a leader
Even if they're not in the leadership team
Employees step up and make a difference
And build other employees' self-esteem

All this creates a culture
When Monday morning comes to be
The team is proud to come to work
For the vision they all see

## *You need empathy to be a leader*

So you want to be a leader
Do you know exactly what that means?
Do you think you have the skills required?
Do you know how to lead a team?

It's much more than being a 'manager'
You need to inspire and motivate
It's not just day-to-day operations
But a vision to communicate

It's about long-term successes
And creating a community
It's building solid relationships
With innovation and creativity

It's a huge responsibility
And it impacts people's lives
Both personally and professionally
As you want your team to thrive

Many people don't have training
And not everyone has the skills
But it's a privilege to lead a team
And ensure they are fulfilled

Can you see someone is hurting
Are you really hearing what they say?
Can you see from another's viewpoint
Or if they're overwhelmed by tragedy?

Do you respect your employees' feelings
Or show that you actually care?
Do you show genuine concern for them?
Do you remind them you are there?

Can you sense someone's emotions
Or imagine what they think?
Can you put yourself in someone else's shoes?
Is empathy your missing link?

You have the power to make a difference
When you lead, or teach or mentor
But if you really want to make a difference
You need empathy to be leader

## *I want you to be my leader*

I want you to be my leader
I want you to hold my hand
I want to put my trust in you
I want you to understand

I want clear expectations
I want time with you each week
To touch base and check progression
We need that time to teach

I want you to be my mentor
I want to look up to you
I want constructive feedback
And I want you to follow through

I want you to listen to me
And really hear what I need to say
Please don't listen to me
Just to give me a reply

I want you to challenge me
So you can help me grow
To have tough conversations
About things that I don't know

I want a strong development
To learn from your experience
I want to have the hard discussions
And to not sit on the fence

I want you to be proud of me
And be an integral part of the team
Even if I make mistakes
I want you to believe in me

I want you to be able to trust me
I want you to have my back
I want you to respect me
And I'll respect you back

I want you to support me
If I need to raise my hand
And tell you there are issues
And for you to lend a helping hand

I want you to ask for my opinion
And listen to what I have to say
That what I do here is important
And tell me, I did great work today!

I don't want toxic behaviour
Or constant negativity
I want to feel appreciated
That will get the best from me

Remember a leader is not just a title
It's about inspiring others
So inspire me to fill my dreams
And let's see what we both discover

I want you to help develop me
I want you to be my teacher
So one day I will fill your shoes
And also be a respected leader

This will help me pay it forward
And I'll mentor all my team
I'll hold their hands like you held mine
And lead them like you led me

# *Do you have a regular check in?*

Do you have a regular check in?
Do you ask employees how they are?
Nothing work related
But just asking 'cause you care

Do you ask how things are personally
Is everything ok?
Is there anything you're struggling with?
How can I help you through your day?

Do you offer staff some guidance
On how they can get some help?
Do you share tools the company offers
So they're not so overwhelmed?

Do you ask them where they are to date
Or what's excited them the most?
Do you tell them you appreciate the work they do
Or try to give them hope?

Do you offer them suggestions
If things might fall behind?
Do you help adjust their schedule
If they're running out of time?

Do you ask them what was hard this week
Of if there's anything they'd like to share?
Do you remind them of work/life balance
Or ensuring their self care?

Do you constantly cancel check ins?
Do you change the conversation?
Which can deflate the employee
And inflate the situation

So remember, as a leader
You need to give your team your time
Set up check ins in your calendar
And ensure you don't decline

### *Being a leader is rewarding*

Being a leader is rewarding
As I mentor and guide my employees
Creating a vision for us to work towards
And putting my team at ease

It's about motivating others
Inspiring my team with enthusiasm
Making them feel valued and included
As they work each day with passion

It's about seeing employees learn and grow
And when they're stepping up
As they follow in my leadership
Instead of giving up

It's about mentoring my employees
To help guide them along the way
To help increase their confidence
And be a role model every day

It's about watching staff move through the ranks
As their new skills come into play
And to see their newfound passion
As they come to work each day

It's about collaboration
And seeing the team all work together
Knowing they work with respect and trust
Even when there is high pressure

It's about motivating my employees
So the team is positive
This brings high productivity
And helps to stop the negative

It's about making hard decisions
And communicating to my team
As we work towards the company goals
This can fuel my self-esteem

But most of all it's about my employees
As I sit back and watch my team
Happy, healthy and working together
As we all grow the company dream

### Not on my watch

Not on my watch
Will bullying be accepted
That behaviour has no place here
And it won't be tolerated

Not on my watch
As I make a promise to myself
I will take good care of all my staff
And their mental health

Not on my watch
Do I want my staff to be in pain
And have the workplace be the cause of it
I won't put them through that strain

Not on my watch
Will I be too blind to see
I will not have a toxic culture
Be my legacy!

## *What employees want*

It's very *simple* what employees want
When they turn up for work each day
They want to trust their company
And feel *respected* in every way

They want strong *communication*
And to come together as a team
This is important to being *successful*
As they build a positive theme

They want a sense of *belonging*
Have everyone work with *integrity*
As they make staff feel *included*
And work with *kindness* and *honesty*

They want to feel that they are *valued*
And *empowered* in their role
They want to be *challenged* in their findings
And have the job not take its toll

They want to have a *mentor*
And be *promoted* within the team
To be *paid well* for the job they do
And to build their *self-esteem*

They want to be *appreciated*
And be *involved* in decisions made
They want to *speak up* when they have to
Without having to be afraid

They want to be able to give *feedback*
And to make sure that they are heard
That there'll be *no repercussions*
Or *without feeling undeterred*

They want to feel *safe* when they make mistakes
It's something we all can do
Mistakes are how we learn and grow
So make it safe to do

They want leaders with *compassion*
And who have *empathy*
Leaders who can be *open minded*
And are always *trustworthy*

So let's make a *safe and healthy workplace*
Where everybody's not so stressed
Where we all come together as a team
Where we can *do what we love best*

So build a people focused *culture*
Where employees want to stay
Because they *have trust and feel respected*
When they come to work each day

## *What companies should want*

Companies want to hire people
Who have skills and experience
But they may not tick all the boxes
Remember, it's not all about their experience

A perfect resume' doesn't ensure the right employee
You need to confirm a cultural fit
Hard skills can be developed
But you want a strong work ethic

They should want staff who show enthusiasm
And a passion for what they do
That they can hit the ground running
And learn the other things to do

It's not all about their education
Many people learn more on the job
They have the desire to make a difference
Because their hunger never stops

They may love to grow a business
Or help their customers every day
They'll do the very best they can
Because their drive won't go away

Many employees are self-motivated
They know what they need to do
That's the reason that you hired them
So let them do what they love to do

Don't hire staff with required skillsets
And then not allow them to be free
Because if you micromanage them
They won't be able to achieve

Each candidate offers something different
With new ideas and experience
They may come from another industry
Where they can show a point of difference

So remember when you're interviewing
There are skills you cannot teach
Work with them on their development
And have success within their reach

## Succession planning

We ensure continuity for our company
So we have a succession plan
We identify successors
And we help their skills expand

This is an important part of business
As it's an ever-changing world
When employees leave organisations
You don't want business to be disturbed

It helps develop and retain staff
As they want a progressional plan
If they can see themselves advance here
There's more chance they'll stay long-term

We've identified crucial positions
And we've assessed our talent pool
Searching for the ones who have the potential
To step up and fill these shoes

We then develop each employee
Based on their skills and expertise
To ensure they'll be successful
As they face this role with ability

We get buy-in from senior leaders
So every leader helps staff progress
It gives employees a future vision
And ensures our company long-term success

We want employees to step up quickly
When another staff member leaves
Especially in leadership positions
As we adapt to problems and opportunities

This all helps to limit disruption
And we support staff who are ambitious
We ensure a smooth transition to leadership
And minimise turmoil to our business

## There is no 'I' in TEAM

A good team is on a common mission
Where everyone understands their roles
Each member trusts and supports each other
And they are committed to company goals

They all have a mutual assurance
And they work collectively
They either win or lose together
Because that's what a team should be

Everyone has their particular tasks to do
And respect will reign surpreme
They collaborate all together
And build each others self-esteem

They can challenge one another
And everyone can share their point of view
Without the fear of being judged
They can feel comfortable to pursue

We use a respectful tone within the workplace
And we all have different perspectives
But we ensure we're open minded
So every viewpoint is effective

Employees all learn and grow together
Which makes them stronger over time
They back each other when they have to
And support each other through hard times

They have a leader who supports them
And always tries to understand
There's no task that is beneath them
They roll their sleeves up and lend a hand

Our team come together Monday mornings
Commiting to grow the company dream
They work happily together
Because there is no 'I' in TEAM

## Inclusion in the workplace

Employees feel included in the workplace
With a sense that they belong
Everything about them is accepted
Regardless of where they're from

We hire a variety of backgrounds
Ensure everyone has the support they need
We provide inclusion training
To ensure all staff succeed

We share ideas and opinions
No-one's afraid to speak their mind
The feeling here is positive
Because everyone is kind

We don't want staff feeling isolated
They belong here in this team
It creates a happy workplace
And increases productivity

We support a safe working environment
With clear communication from the top
We ask for staff's opinion
Because we value skills they've got

We celebrate diversity
Through activities and events
So we learn each other's backgrounds
And how each one represents

We want staff to feel connected
So no-one ever feels displaced
It builds trust with our employees
By having inclusion in the workplace

## *Autonomy in the workplace*

We offer autonomy in the workplace
Give employees freedom to do their work
So they can decide what works best for them
And shows you trust them to do their work

Many roles can work varied hours
Not everything needs to be 9-5
Giving your team some independence
Can help your business thrive

There's many reasons it's important
It reduces stress and improves morale
You have a happier workplace
When employees have some more control

It increases employee engagement
And also productivity
Employees can be more creative
When you promote workplace autonomy

We give clear goals and objectives
Provide the resources that they need
Trust employees to make decisions
Reward and recognise autonomy

Employees that are given freedom to work on projects
Where they have an increased passion
And encouraged to be creative
Will have increased satisfaction

When companies focus on autonomy
And staff can make decisions for themselves
And they're not being micromanaged
Helps employees not feel so overwhelmed

We ensure a safe space for employees
And it's safe to speak up when there's mistakes
Mistakes are how we learn and grow
And what a difference this can make

Many employees have to juggle
Different things within their life
They have commitments outside the workplace
So give them the chance to live their life

If employees have some freedom
And choose the hours that they work
They can create a work/life balance
And be more engaging in their work

Working with autonomy in the workplace
Has many benefits for your company
As it allows your team the chance to thrive
To become 'best-in-class' within your industry

## It takes a village

'It takes a village to raise a child'
As entire communities interact
They help the child to learn and grow
It's a saying from decades back

Communities help to care for the child
They are present and they support
They are an active part of the child's life
Growing in a safe and healthy environment

But when the child is not embraced
It's a painful thing to see
If they are not accepted
Or rejected from the community

It seems a little like the workplace
As leaders support and guide their team
As everybody in the village
Helps support the company dream

But when there's toxicity in the workplace
Nobody can learn and grow
The village learns what not to do
And frustrations will constantly show

So let's make sure everyone's included
Embrace everybody on the team
Create a safe and happy village
Where kindness will reign supreme

## It's more than tea and biscuits

It's more than tea and biscuits
For the wellbeing of your staff
Your employees are your biggest asset
Where they work on your behalf

Your team takes care of your customers
With dedication and empathy
Which in return, looks after business
But can drain staff mentally

There's some things that staff want in return
And it's that they want your trust
To feel safe in this company
And be respected, is a must

We need to foster change and culture
We need a positive place to work
We want staff to feel supported
And valued where they work

Together, we can make this change
Be the place everyone wants to be
Have candidates knocking on your door
For the great company they can see

Let's have open communication
Foster an environment of trust
Make people feel they can speak up
About their mental health

Let's encourage work/life harmony
Inspire to unplug after work
Let's set clear and stable boundaries
Turn phones and email off after work

Let's get serious on resources
And encourage much self-care
Offer health days and wellness programs
And remember EAP

Let's acknowledge staff all deal with
So many things in life
Extra support can make a difference
And help someone change their life

Let's adapt to change in working needs
Flexible hours and hybrid models
And support the various needs required
We can't all work in a busy office

Let's remember to appreciate
The hard work that our staff do
A simple 'thank you' can boost morale
And make them feel so valued

Let's remember to include everyone
We want all employees to have a voice
To show that everyone's included
And they all have a choice

Let's not take the team for granted
Create a happy and healthy theme
Where everyone can come to work
And be respected as a team

Mental health in the workplace needs to improve
Which in return, is good for business
Let's make mental health a priority
But it's much more than tea and biscuits

## Improve your staff retention

You should invest in your employees
With training and development
Making them feel informed and valued
It's time and money that's well spent

Create growth opportunities
And reward staff along the way
Create a positive culture
Ensure communication, always

Ensure you have some mentors
That can help encourage staff
We all need someone to guide us
But they need to be fit for the task

Support cross functional improvements
And support your team's mental health
Provide them valuable resources
To help build up their strength

Show staff empathy and kindness
And that you actually care
Remind them that you are a team
And if they need you, you are there

Have some team activities
Encouraging staff to socialise
So they get to know each other
And build connections that can thrive

When you invest in your employees
You provide resources that they crave
So they can continue to develop skills
And bring more confidence to their day

Create succession planning
So staff can learn and grow
They have a development goal to work towards
And increased excitement will then show

This all increases staff performance
With engagement and interaction
It helps build a better workplace
And improves your staff retention

## *Create a workplace etiquette*

We need to set up boundaries in the workplace
So we can help manage our day
Ensure we're not working back to back
With no breaks throughout the day

We need to manage work expectations
As so many staff are overworked
With unrealistic expectations
Which has an impact on their health

We need to establish standard hours
Times to start and times to finish
Establishing these core hours
Will help some pressure to diminish

Limit after hours communication
Keep it to a minimum
Unless something is truly urgent
It can wait until the morning

Remember when sending emails
Don't send it to the world
Choose who really needs TO: see it
And who needs to be CC'd:

Make sure it's very clear to all
If an action is required
Otherwise there's duplication
And it can then get staff off side

Now let's talk about those meetings
Are they really all required?
They can be a huge time waster
Make sure staff are needed and inspired

When you book a meeting
Invite only those who are essential
Include with it an agenda
So staff can confirm they are integral

So when staff receive a meeting invite
They can see what's to be discussed
Sometimes they don't need to be there
And another employee does

Please note when booking meetings
Check employees' calendars and you'll see
They may already be back to back that day
So make sure you give them time to breathe

Please don't book meetings over meetings
This seems to happen all the time
It's so annoying and frustrating
And most staff should just decline

Don't book meetings during lunchtime
Remember all staff need a break
They may use this time to eat and exercise
So please don't make that mistake

Please don't book meetings after hours
Remember staff have a life outside of work
They may already have things scheduled
They shouldn't have to cancel due to work

Make sure you keep your schedule
Ensuring you don't go over time
Remember, your priority might not be there's
They may have other things on their mind

All this helps protect your workday
And protects your personal time
It helps to protect your energy
Your wellbeing and your life

## Remote work

Let's have a remote work conversation
As the whole world has now changed
Since the aftereffects of COVID
Our work structure has rearranged

As we all had to work from home
Many people struggled with that at first
But many people also embraced it
Because they could see how much it worked

Remember COVID changed us
We may now function differently
We may not be able to work the way we used to
The office might cause anxiety

Employees can be so very productive
Working in their own environment
Which promotes a sense of purpose
Boosts self-esteem and confidence

It encourages healthy habits
That can improve your mental health
It can reduce stress and anxiety
As it contributes to work/life balance

It allows staff more time with family
Or more time on their own health
Which can enhance their creativity
And increase the ability to excel

Many staff don't need to work 9-5
That is so old school
And just because staff work from home
Doesn't mean they're breaking rules

We need to change the old school mindset
That they're not working if not at work
You need to ensure you trust your staff
Because most are showing you their worth

You can see the work is being done
You can see staff attend 'Team' meetings
Just because you can't see them at their desk
Doesn't mean they bludge the system

You can see how much staff appreciate
Not wasting time in all that traffic
This can waste many hours of their day
And make their mood fanatic

Employees can achieve so much when they work from home
If they're not constantly interrupted
I know side conversations at work can be valuable
But they also cause disruption

Staff can lose time working from the office
When others come to sit and talk
Or they get called into last-minute meetings
That takes them away from work

If staff don't get enough done in the office
And then they have a long drive home
They may have to log on after hours
To make up for that wasted time

This may now affect their homelife
Their time with kids and family
Don't be the cause of personal issues
Support them with what they want to achieve

If you can work together with their timelines
Of dealing with life outside of work
Staff will appreciate you so much more
And be more excited about their work

So please just learn to trust your staff
When they want to work from home
All the proof is in the results they show
And highlights work is getting done

You may want the face to face of teamwork
And have staff back working in the office
But if you have a toxic culture
Staff won't want to be within the office

So find a balanced hybrid model
Remember one size does not fit all
Trust and communication is so vital
To ensure the right result for all

## *The importance of self-care*

When everything is overwhelming
Just take a step back and breathe
Take some time out for yourself
And help your mind to heal

Do some things that make you happy
A beach walk, some sun, some air
Take some time to just reflect each day
And remember your self-care

Sometimes you need to allow yourself
To let it out and have a cry
Don't bottle things up inside yourself
That's not good for you or I

Go and get back into nature
Take a long walk or hug a tree
Just remember to take some time for you
For the difference you will see

Spend some time with loved ones
Do the things you love the most
Learn to say 'no' when you're extended
And start a new approach

Take some time to do some reading
A great book or poetry
Go and take a bike ride
And feel your hair blow in the breeze

Download an app onto your phone
Reminding you to take a break
To slow down and hear some music
Or do yoga at daybreak

Learn to set up boundaries
Speak up if you need help
Ensure short breaks and take a breath
It's vital for your mental health

## Remember, it's more than tea and biscuits!

Remember, it's more than tea and biscuits for the wellbeing of your employees. Benefits can assist to attract and retain staff. Here's a selection of benefits I've noticed in recent job advertisements:

**Compensation**
Competitive salary, bonuses, spot bonuses, share options, profit sharing.

**Benefits**
Healthcare, extra holiday leave, ability to purchase leave, mental health days, day off for your birthday, parental leave, carer's leave, employee referral program, retirement planning, discounts and memberships, staff discounts.

**Health and wellbeing**
Employee assistance program (EAP), gym memberships, support programs, pets welcome, massage in the office, yoga days, wellbeing allowance, flexible working arrangements, interactive wellbeing apps, casual work days.

**Training and education**
Personal and online training programs, leadership training, mental health in the workplace training, professional development books, eBooks and podcasts. Mentorship training for formal mentorship program. Formal buddy program. Succession planning for growth opportunities.

**Awards (incorporate Visa card, points, shares, etc)**
Multiple monthly, quarterly and yearly awards where all staff have the ability to win. Celebrate successes along the way.

### Some newer rewards types

Offer holiday vouchers to ensure all staff get the break they need or offer a Visa card or holiday option depending in individual preference. Offer QR code access for coffee to be delivered to employees' desks when they are working from the office.

### Individuals option

Why not work out the desired benefit program for your company and incorporate an 'individuals option'? This could be three or four benefits that employees could choose for themselves as different things motivate different people.

### Other options – think outside the square

What other benefits can you introduce to your company that will make a significant difference? Maybe even have a brainstorming session with your employees to understand what will drive them the most. There may be a few key options that will significantly motivate them. Get to know your employees and find out what is happening in your employees' lives and see if there is a way you can support them. What are your company dynamics? Are there many working mothers or single parents? Potential offering could be childcare assistance, child tutoring or a house cleaner. What about paying for education for employees' children or the employees themselves for activities outside of school and work. Examples are: a sports activity, learning a new language or musical instrument.

Think outside the square and remember that if there are great benefits and you are looking after your employees' mental and physical health, and potentially their family in some way, they will talk about your company more and more in a positive way, becoming great brand ambassadors.

*However, while having amazing benefits is definitely attractive, if the culture is toxic, the toxicity outweighs the benefits and they are no longer attractive.*

*It must be a balance of a positive culture with amazing benefits to attract and retain staff.*

## How the recruitment process affects the company culture

The recruitment process can be a root cause of toxic culture because toxic people have been able to join the company in the first place. The best way to ensure you don't have a toxic culture is to try and prevent it. So, how do you weed out toxic candidates before they join the company? What do you look for? How do you ask the right questions? What type of questions do you ask?

There are some questions you can ask in an interview and their responses can help determine a candidate's behaviour. This should give you an indication if a candidate's behaviour could be toxic. Recruiters could ask questions that will show potential red flags in behaviours. These might be fairly standard questions, but listen to how the candidate responds to these questions.

- Tell me about a time when you had to deal with a difficult colleague. How did you handle it?
- How would you describe your ideal work environment?
- How do you collaborate with the team?
- How do you handle criticism and feedback?
- What are your career goals?
- Why are you interested in this position?
- What specifically can you offer this role?
- Why should we hire you?

How did the candidate respond?

- Did they respond in a positive and constructive manner?
- Did they take responsibility for their own actions?
- Did they show a willingness to learn and grow?

- Did they focus on being a team player?
- Did they show unrealistic expectations?
- Did they seem to have difficulty working with others?
- Did they blame others if things went wrong?
- Did they have a negative or aggressive attitude?
- Did they focus on their own success or was it a team success?

Other questions could be:

- What do you think your weaknesses are? How would you go about improving them?
- What skills do you lack that might be required for this position?
- What skills do you think you can improve on?

These types of questions allow the candidate to be very exposed. Will they claim they actually have weaknesses or they need to make some improvements because they are not good at something, or will they claim they know everything? We all have strengths and weaknesses, so if they say they don't have weaknesses, or claim to know everything, that could be a red flag.

Ask them, 'What do you need to know about us to determine if we are a good fit for you?'

Also, take note of the questions they are asking you. Are their questions focused on the company and the team, or are they focused on themselves only?

Remember, you are interviewing a candidate to ensure they are the right fit for the culture and the team. This person will have an impact on your team and your business. You are not just ticking a box.

Hiring a toxic person can also bring a whole lot of good work undone. Sometimes, it can take just one bad egg to bring everything down, so it's best to do everything to prevent it from happening in the first place.

There's no 'one size fits all' when interviewing for the right fit for your company and these are only a few examples. But hopefully, it gives you something to think about.

## The link from culture to performance

There is a strong link between culture and performance in organisations. Creating a positive culture leads to higher employee engagement, productivity and innovation. Likewise, a negative culture can lead to low morale, high staff turnover and low productivity.

A positive company culture will significantly impact business outcomes. It can influence employee engagement, productivity and innovation. In a positive environment, people naturally do more.

**Employee engagement:**
Employees who are engaged in their work are motivated, creative and productive. A positive culture can promote employee engagement by providing employees with a sense of purpose, teamwork, learning, belonging, growth, and fun, all while feeling they're in a safe environment.

**Employee productivity:**
Employees who are happy and fulfilled with their jobs are more productive. A positive culture can promote employee productivity by creating a supportive and collaborative work environment. Employees can also feel they have personal and professional growth with a sense of achievement.

**Employee innovation:**
Employees who feel they are in a safe environment and encouraged to share their thoughts and ideas or take risks, are more innovative. A positive culture can promote employee innovation by creating a culture of excitement, motivation, learning, developing, research, and experimentation.

A positive work culture has a major impact on how employees think, feel and perform at work. If the company is looking after their employees, then naturally employees want to do the best they possibly can for the company. This can lead to better financial performance and overall success for the company. It will also increase personal financial outcomes for employees through commissions, bonuses and awards.

The market will also hear about the positive work culture of your company, where top candidates will want to come and work. And that's what you want—to have candidates knocking down your door to work for your company.

## *Performance reviews are so outdated!*

Performance reviews are so outdated
As employees perservere
There's got to be a better way
Than ticking a box once or twice a year

Reviews can be so stressful
For both managers and staff
If giving negative feedback
Because work isn't up to task

If someone has a toxic manager
How can it be fair?
If the employee is doing all they can
But the manager doesn't care!

Most often there's no follow up
To check in or give support
So how is this effective
If there is no support?

What process do you have in place
To make it fair across the board
If staff have issues with their manager
To have all avenues explored?

It's not fair when staff get marked down
Because the manager cannot see
This employee is doing all they can
To support the company

This review is about performance
Which links to raises, bonuses and promotions
It affects our employees' livelihoods
And also their emotions

So, we'll work out a better way
To assess our staff's performance
Because ticking this review box each year
Doesn't give staff much assurance

These conversations increase engagement
Help with trust and productivity
They detect development and progress
So we'll ensure they happen every week

## *How to manage change effectively*

Change can have an impact on performance
With many challenges from your decision
You need to ensure some proper planning
To ensure a smooth transition

There may be a communication breakdown
Or loss of productivity
You might find staff have resistance
Change doesn't always come so easily

There might be an increase in absence
Or a breakdown within the team
You need an implementation plan
So you can build staff's self-esteem

Employees may not understand what's happening
They'll be worried about their job
It can cause stress and anxiety
And their apprehension may not stop

Employees can struggle with change management
And the disruption it can cause
There might also be external factors
That might cause your team to pause

But change can be positive in the workplace
It can motivate and increase morale
It can bring new ways of working
But the team need the rationale

You may need a different way of working
You may need a change of process
Organisational change may be required
For the policies you'll address

So when there's change within the business
Plan and communicate to the team
Reward for good behaviours through the changes
To help uplift the staff's esteem

## *Let's spread a little workplace kindness*

Let's spread a little workplace kindness
We work together every day
Let's make it a happy place to be
Let's help brighten someone's day

Kindness shows that you are valued
By your colleagues and your team
It highlights your belonging
And it helps build your self-esteem

Let's appreciate each other
For the great work that they do
Remember, they do so much more
Than the task they do for you!

Why not bake some cup cakes
And share them with the team
It's the little acts of kindness
That create a positive theme

Let's notice team mates under pressure
And ask them if they need a hand
Surprise them with a cup of coffee
Let them know you understand

Why not highlight when they need a break
And take them for a walk
To get some fresh air and some breathing space
It will allow some time to talk

Tell somebody, 'thank you'
For the great job that they do
Those two words make such a difference
And bring so much gratitude

Kindness can be contagious
It can increase productivity
It helps create a positive culture
And helps make work a happy place to be

So let's spread some kindness in the workplace
Compliment your colleagues along the way
For these little acts of kindness
Can brighten someone's day

## Great leadership training must-haves

You shouldn't put someone into a leadership role without training in leadership. Leadership is an important responsibility and can have a direct impact on employees' careers, their personal lives and the success of the company. Here are some examples of leadership courses that all leaders should complete. Leaders also need their ongoing development plan.

If you are committed to being a good leader, you need to put in the effort to develop the necessary skill set. If you are now managing people, you need the right training and skills to manage a team effectively. People are the biggest assets of the company and you are guiding them on their current role, their future and their career path, which has an impact on them personally. So it's imperative you have the right skill set to manage people.

**Leadership courses**
- Communication
- Motivation
- Decision making
- Problem solving
- Teamwork
- Building high performance teams
- Thought leadership
- Lead with heart
- Psychological safety in the workplace
- Succession planning
- Leading with Emotional Intelligence
- Critical Thinking Skills
- Dealing with Difficult People or Conversations
- Work/Life Balance and Healthy Work Boundaries
- Critical Stress Debriefing
- Mental Health First Aid (ALL people managers)

- Bullying and harrassment in the workplace. Ensure you and your team *can* see the signs!

**From Linda Crockett – The Canadian Institute of Workplace Bullying Resources**
*All leaders should have mandatory trauma-informed training on prevention, intervention, repair, and recovery options for workplace psychological harassment and psychological violence. This workplace abuse is not just about policies and procedures; this is about human beings who suffer moderate to severe psychological and physical injuries due to the cumulative effect of this type of abuse. You do not have to be a psychologist, but it is imperative that leaders (including HR) stop making ill-informed comments and gestures causing secondary harm to these employees. Trauma-informed training provides leaders and staff with skills that will reduce harm, improve recovery time, retain hard working employees, and save costs. This is just good business common sense.*

We know people don't leave companies, they leave bad cultures or bad managers. Having effective people management skills can increase productivity, employee morale and reduce staff turnover. Any person in a management role managing people must have people management training. If you don't, you are setting yourself up to fail and you can have a negative impact on your employees' mental health and even their lives.

**People management**
- Fundamentals of people management
- Effective communication for people managers
- Motivating and engaging employees
- Performance management
- Conflict resolution
- Diversity and inclusion

- Coaching and mentoring
- Continuing to grow your own personal development will help you become an effective people manager and leader. You are also leading by example for continual learning, which will resonate with your staff.

**Soft skill requirements**

To be an effective leader, soft skills are essential to build strong relationships and create a positive working environment. If employees are promoted, it's not always noticeable when they have previously been a single contributor, but how do you know they have the soft skills to be responsible for the next step in their career, which includes managing people?

Here is an example of soft skills for effective leadership:

**Empathy:** Leaders need to be able to understand and relate to the needs and feelings of others. They need to be able to put themselves in someone else's shoes and try to imagine the situation as their own. This allows them to motivate their teams and build strong relationships, and also create a positive and inclusive work environment. Empathy is also significant for managing difficult situations and resolving conflict. Listening is a big part of empathy, paying attention to what's being said and observing body language. Ask questions to clarify and show that you are listening and interested.

**Communication:** Leaders need to be able to communicate clearly, concisely and persuasively. They need to be able to adapt their communication technique to different situations. Communication is essential for building trust, motivating team members and resolving issues quickly. Ask engaging questions and really listen to what's being said. Don't just give a reply. And again, understand body language. Ask questions to clarify and show that you are listening and interested.

**Adaptability:** In this ever-changing world, leaders need to be able to adapt to change quickly and be comfortable with their decisions. They need to think on their feet, adjust their strategies and be open to new ideas. Adaptability is crucial for leading organisations through times of change and uncertainty. Challenge yourself to try new things and maybe even step outside your comfort zone to see how you cope with change. Be open to new ideas and different perspectives from your team.

1. **Motivation:** Leaders need to be able to motivate and inspire their teams to achieve both personal and company goals. This includes being able to set clear expectations and goals, provide constructive feedback and recognise achievements. Motivation is critical for creating a high-performing team and achieving company success. Break down larger goals into achievable pieces, so it's not overwhelming. And show visuals of improvements to the team to keep the momentum. Find inspiration from other people and read about how they overcame their own challenges.

2. **Integrity:** Leaders must be ethical and have strong moral values. They need to be honest, trustworthy and fair. Integrity is essential for building trust, earning respect and maintaining a positive reputation. Identify and understand your core values and ensure you constantly work towards them. If you make commitments, make sure you honour them. Treat others the way you want to be treated—with respect and dignity—even if you disagree with something.

3. **Self-awareness:** Leaders need to be self-aware of their own strengths and weaknesses and be able to identify their own areas for improvement. Self-awareness is essential for personal growth, effective leadership and building strong relationships. Practice self-reflection and take time to really

think about your thoughts, how you've acted and how you've treated people. Do you need to make changes? Also seek feedback from colleagues and understand your actions and choices and how you might improve them.

Before promoting an employee into a role that has people management responsibility, why not create a task or a project they need to manage to see what soft skills come through in the process. You may have two great candidates, but one may also shine through with their soft skills, making them a better candidate for people management. With the other candidate, you can now help them develop these skills for the next opportunity.

Continuing to grow your own personal development will help you become an effective people manager and leader. You are also leading by example for continual learning, which will resonate with your staff.

Other resources available for ongoing development include:

- Reading books on leadership, and taking webinars and online courses.
- Seeking out opportunities to lead. This could involve volunteering to lead a project at work or joining a committee or group out of work.
- Pulling your sleeves up and getting in and helping. Offering help when required and leading by example.
- Understanding the needs and ensuring you know how other departments operate to ensure collaboration and productivity.
- Asking your manager for feedback and identifying areas that might need improvement.
- Asking staff who report directly to you what you could do better to help them as their leader.

- Finding a coach and mentor who will guide you and support you on your leadership journey. This needs to be someone you look up to and someone who is already respected and experienced in a leadership role. They don't necessarily need to be working in the same company.

## Great leadership reads

*7 Rituals of the Resilient Leader eBook* by Graeme Cowan

*At the Heart of Leadership: How To Get Results with Emotional Intelligence* by Joshua Freedman and Peter Salovey

*A World of Difference: Leading in Global Markets with Cultural Intelligence* by Felicity Menzies

*Burn Bright Not Out: The Playful Guide to Recharging* by Alicia Ann Wade

*Co-Bully NO MORE: And become Co-Dependent Free* by Judith Carmody

*Dare to Lead: Brave Work. Tough Conversations. Whole Hearts* by Brene' Brown

*Essential Questions to GROW Your Team: A Toolkit of Coaching Conversations for Managers and Leaders* by Kathryn Jackson

*Give and Take: A Revolutionary Approach to Success* by Adam Grant

*Good to Great: Why Some Companies Make the Leap... and Others Don't* by Jim Collins

*Head, Heart and Guts: How the World's Best Companies Develop Complete Leaders* by David L. Dotlich, Peter C. Cairo and Stephen H. Rhinesmith

*Heal the World with Kindness: Messages of Hope and Kindness* by Sibel Terhaar

*Heart-Centered Leadership: Lead Well, Live Well* by Susan Steinbrecher and Dr Joel Bennett

*How Can You Not See The Signs? For leaders to notice the signs of a toxic culture. For employees to notice toxic behaviour* by Jo Woodhouse

*Lead from the Heart: Transformational Leadership for the 21st Century* by Mark C. Crowley

*Leader Awakened: Why accepting adversity drives power and freedom* by Samreen McGregor

*Leaders Eat Last: Why Some Teams Pull Together and Others Don't* by Simon Sinek

*Leadership and Self-Deception: Getting Out of the Box* by The Arbinger Institute

*Leadership Wisdom from the Monk Who Sold His Ferrari* by Robin S. Sharma

*Practical Leadership in Nursing and Health Care: A Multi-Professional Approach* by Dr Suzanne Henwood

*Primal Leadership: Learning to Lead with Emotional Intelligence* by Daniel Goleman, Richard Boyatzis and Annie McKee

*Resilience at Work: Practical Tools for Career Success* by Kathryn Jackson

*Start with Why: How Great Leaders Inspire Everyone to Take Action* by Simon Sinek

*The 7 Habits of Highly Effective People* by Stephen R. Covey

*The Elephant in the Boardroom: Getting Mentally Fit for Work* by Graeme Cowan

*The Five Dysfunctions of a Team: A Leadership Fable* by Patrick M. Lencioni

*The Inspirational Leader: Inspire Your Team To Believe In The impossible* by Gifford Thomas

*Unlearning Silence: How to speak your mind, unleash talent and lead with courage* by Elaine Lin Hering

*UNLIKE A BOSS: Positive People Leadership Skills You Wish Your Manager Had* by Alexander N. Andrews

*Unlock The Hidden Leader: Become The Leader You Were Destined To Be* by Gifford Thomas

*Who Moved My Cheese* by Dr Spencer Johnson

As part of an ongoing leadership development program, why not create a 'leadership book club', where all leaders in the company must read these books and discuss as a team. That way, positive leadership and change are being instilled into the team.

The leadership team can then move forward together. The discussion could include how they have put these books into action, what they have learned, what they have changed, what they have or will do differently as an individual and as a team.

Remember, all 'leaders' should be on the same train, so everyone needs to embrace this journey, stay on the train and work together, or they need to get off and find another train.

## *Creating a psychologically safe workplace*

If you're serious about taking action to ensure your organisation is able to prevent, support and respond to mental health risks, it's best to use people and organisations who are experts in this field, who focus on mental health and leading wellbeing in the workplace. If team members are struggling and open up, it can also create a supportive environment.

Different countries, states and regions may also have government offered training courses. Your human resources department should also be able to source this information for you.

When people want to make change, sometimes they don't know where to start. I have recently connected with some absolutely amazing people and organisations who are experts in their field and passionate about making a difference to wellbeing in the workplace and lives in general. They all offer valuable services and support to your organisations, assisting you to make a psychologically safe workplace.

The following pages offer you a wealth of knowledge and experience from people who are truly making an impact in creating a healthy work environment.

# Resources for creating a psychologically safe workplace

## Australia

### Alexander N. Andrews
Leadership consultant (specialising in cultural transformation), mentor, keynote speaker and author of bestseller *UNLIKE A BOSS*. Alexander is based in Australia, however, offers support globally.
www.unlikeaboss.com
Contact via: alexander@unlikeaboss.com.au

### Alice Taugs
### Empowered by Alice
Alice Taugs, founder of Empowered by Alice & Retreat a Little, specialises in empowering individuals to rediscover their core values and strengths, enhancing clarity, confidence and resilience. This work has led her to offer holistic organisational transformation to cultivate healthy work cultures and combat burnout.

With over twenty years in the global pharmaceutical and medical device industry, and insights gained from a personal health crisis in 2019, Alice's journey into psychology and leadership has equipped her with powerful tools for authentic living. Alice is based in Australia; however, she offers support globally.
www.retreatalittle.com

### Alicia Ann Wade
Alicia is your source of motivation for unforgettable events. Alicia isn't just a speaker; she's a powerhouse of inspiration, a master of connection and a beacon of positivity.

Whether it's team meetings, conferences, workshops or special events, Alicia is the speaker you've been seeking to ignite motivation.

With a compelling narrative of resilience, tragedy to triumph, test to testimony, and victim to victor, Alicia demonstrates that the impossible can indeed be possible. Her journey from learning difficulties to becoming an Educator of the Year, International #1 Best Selling Author, International Life Coach of The Year, and receiving many accolades, showcases her exceptional achievements.

Alicia offers one-hour motivational speaking sessions tailored to your needs, and her pricing is determined in consultation with the company or business owner. Additionally, she provides one-on-one sound healing therapy, effective in addressing conditions like stress, anxiety, high blood pressure, depression, sleep disorders, pain, and autism.

For a unique group experience, Alicia conducts a two-hour Gratitude Group Sound Healing session, infusing lightness and fun while sharing the importance of sound healing and the practice of gratitude. Reach out to Alicia for a new modality of mindfulness in your workplace or organisation.
www.linkedin.com/in/alicia-ann-wade-10397592
Contact via: info@thegratitudemethod.com.au

**Anna Feringa**
**Anna Feringa Consulting Pty Ltd**
Anna Feringa is a workplace mental health consultant, author, trainer and international speaker.
www.annaferinga.com.au
Contact via: info@annaferinga.com.au

**Beyond Blue Support Service**
Phone: 1300 224 636
www.beyondblue.org.au/mental-health/workplace-bullying-harassment

## Black Dog Institute
Backed by research, and delivered by experts, Black Dog Institute offer a range of training workshops, eLearning programs and presentations to develop skills to build better mental health at work.
www.blackdoginstitute.org.au/education-services/workplaces

## Dr Nathalie Martinek PhD
Dr Nathalie Martinek is a narcissism hacker, consultant, interpersonal conflict analyst, anti-bullying strategist, author, educator, speaker, group facilitator, and coach. She works with victims and perpetrators of narcissistic behaviour and teams to prevent and facilitate recovery from burnout, moral injury and bullying-induced trauma through coaching, mentoring and bespoke workshop facilitation.

She supports individuals and teams to develop interpersonal skills that enable leadership, psychological safety, conflict resolution, and functional relationships. Nathalie is based in Australia and provides services globally.
www.drnathaliemartinek.com
Contact via: hello@drnathaliemartinek.com

## Felicity Menzies
## Include-Empower
Felicity is the principal consultant and CEO of Include-Empower, a Sydney-based global diversity and inclusion consultancy founded in 2012 with expertise encompassing respect at work, trauma-informed practice, inclusive leadership, unconscious bias, cultural intelligence and inclusion, gender equity, and empowering professional women.

Felicity is an accredited facilitator with the Cultural Intelligence Centre and is the author of *A World of Difference: Leading in Global Markets with Cultural Intelligence.* Felicity is a regular contributor to business publications, including *AICD, Forbes,*

*Business Insider, Business First, Acuity, Inhouse Counsel, and People Management.* In 2017, Felicity was awarded Fellow of Chartered Accountants Australia and New Zealand for her work in Diversity and Inclusion and has a Bachelor in Arts (Psychology) and a Bachelor in Commerce. Felicity is currently undertaking a Juris Doctor at the University of Sydney.

In 2021, Felicity's expertise in facilitating high-profile cultural change programs supported her engagement by The Premier's Department NSW (formerly The Department of Premier and Cabinet NSW) to deliver Respect at Work training for NSW ministers and staff as a key recommendation of the Goward Review. In 2022, Felicity's expertise was further recognised when she was appointed by the NSW Parliament to deliver Respect at Work training as a key recommendation of the Broderick Review. Felicity is based in Australia and offers support globally.
www.cultureplusconsulting.com

**Gerard Beven**
**Head of Mental Health & Wellbeing**
**HSE Global**
HSE Global is a leading consultancy organisation specialising in workplace health, safety, environment, and wellbeing. HSE Global is one of the largest providers of mental health first aid globally and provides consulting expertise to support the development of sustainable strategic wellbeing programs. HSE Global has offices in Australia, NZ and the USA, and they service customers globally.
www.hseglobal.com/mental-health
Contact via: healthwellbeing@hseglobal.com

**GOTCHA4LIFE**
**Building mental fitness, together**
Gotcha4Life is a not-for-profit foundation on a mission to inspire and enable all Australians to take action to build their mental fitness so that no-one worries alone.

They develop and deliver preventative programs, workshops and resources, which provide schools, sports clubs, workplaces, and community groups with the skills to build emotional muscles, strengthen social connection and encourage help-seeking behaviour so they are better equipped to get through life's ups and downs.
www.gotcha4life.org

**Graeme Cowan**
**Graeme Cowan Enterprises**
Team Resilience Speaker - Helping managers and teams to be more caring and resilient
Australian Enterprise Awards Winner 2023 – Best Workplace Mental Health Training Organisation APAC
Co-founder WECARE365, Founding Director R U OK?
The Caring CEO Podcast
www.graemecowan.com.au
www.wecare365.com.au
Contact via: graeme@graemecowan.com.au

**Mental Health First Aid Australia**
www.mhfa.com.au
Contact via: mhfa@mhfa.com.au
Contact via: +61 3 9079 0200

**Michelle Boundy**
**Founder, She Inspires Me**
Michelle is an accomplished professional with over thirty years' experience working in government. She is highly educated and a subject matter expert on workplace wellbeing & culture. She has won several awards, including Regional and State Work Health & Safety Champion, the Workcover Outstanding Achievements in Work Health & Safety (Wellbeing) and the prestigious National 'Light Up Award' for Outstanding Achievement in WHS & Wellbeing for the Australian Public Service in November 2022.

She has implemented several highly successful community initiatives, including The Elephant in the Room during Mental Health Month in October 2022, raising over $26,000 for Lifeline. In March 2023, she founded She Inspires Me, which celebrates the contributions and achievements women are making in our community. The #tellyourstory initiative empowers women to share their stories with others to raise awareness of the issues women face in our society to create change in this country.

Michelle's Empower Me Mentoring (for individuals) is designed to equip you with the tools and support necessary to enhance your life. This program provides personalised one-on-one mentoring with Michelle, tailored to meet your specific needs and goals. It focuses on your strengths and aims to help you achieve both your personal and professional aspirations.

Michelle is highly regarded and respected across government and is admired nationally for her unique community projects raising awareness on kindness, mental health, workplace wellbeing, and her genuine desire to make a difference in the lives of others.

Empower Me provides corporate wellbeing programs that help companies identify potential risks, create and implement plans to mitigate them, and enhance their workplace culture. Through regular communication and consultation with employees, they are actively engaged in the decision-making process and have the ability to identify and control risks in the workplace. Consistent monitoring and review of potential risks is essential. Furthermore, employees' awareness of their work, health and safety responsibilities can be improved through education and training.
www.sheinspiresmeaustralia.com
Contact via: michelle@sheinspiresmeaustralia.com

**Sophie Bretag**
**Metta Leaders**
Sophie Bretag, award winning and globally published HR consultant and kindness expert, is the CEO and founder of Metta Leaders. She combines her extensive experience as an executive HR and EQ practitioner with happiness coaching, positive psychology, meditation, breathwork, forest bathing therapy, and women's leadership connection circle facilitation.

Sophie provides contemporary and practical ways to create more happiness and wellbeing in workplaces seeking transformation and she is currently writing her first book on kind leadership. Sophie is based in Australia and supports her clients globally.
www.mettaleaders.com
Contact via: info@mettaleaders.com

**Traci Carse**
**TC Psychology**
Traci is an organisational psychologist (specialising in psychosocial risk management and mental health education), consultant, coach, keynote speaker, and ASIST (suicide intervention skills trainer). Traci is based in Australia; however, she offers support to clients globally.
www.tcpsychology.net
Contact via: traci@tcpsychology.net

# Canada

**Linda Crockett MSW, RSW, SEP, CPPA**
**Founder, The Canadian Institute of Workplace Bullying Resources, Canada (for profit)**
Linda Crockett is a specialist in trauma-informed approaches to workplace harassment, bullying, violence solutions prevention,

intervention, repair/recovery, consulting, coaching, mentoring, training, and counselling. Linda is based in Canada; however, she supports clients globally.
www.instituteofworkplacebullyingresources.ca
www.linkedin.com/in/ciwpbr

**The Canadian Institute of Workplace Harassment and Violence (not for profit)**
www.workplaceharassment.ca

## Germany

**Kasia Musur**
**VENT (VENT about the toxic boss)**
Kasia Musur is the founder of VENT. VENT is a collaboration hub developing solutions to reduce the impact of toxic leadership on individuals, communities, businesses, and the environment. VENT offers collaboration opportunities, creating tailor-made workshops and tech solutions, addressing the issue of toxic leadership in a workplace.
www.toxicleadershipvent.com
www.linkedin.com/in/katarzyna-kasia-musur
Contact via: kasia@toxicleadershipvent.com

## Ireland

**Judy Carmody CPA, PGD, (MA Leadership in Workplace Health and Wellbeing)**
Judith is an Irish author, researcher and educator with knowledge on the dynamics and contexts of leadership and wellbeing in the workplace. Judith's work focuses on the prevention and intervention of bullying in the workplace. Her books, *Co-Bully No More* and *Unwrap the Gift of YOU* are based on her experiential knowledge and evidence-based research. She is an actively engaged advocate of leadership, safety, health and wellbeing in the workplace.

Judith penned an exceptional book, *Co-Bully No More,* upon which she based her powerful presentation THE POWER OF YOU to a standing ovation at the Professional Women Network International Conference in Kentucky, USA in 2018. She gave an equally impactful presentation at Kerry's first Health & Wellbeing Week. In June 2019, she presented The Bystander(s) at the World Anti-Bullying Forum in Dublin.

www.judithcarmody.com
www.linkedin.com/in/judith-carmody-author
Contact via: carmody.judy@gmail.com

## New Zealand

**Blueprint for Learning**
Blueprint for Learning is one of New Zealand's largest training providers in mental health and addiction and provides a range of workshops.
www.blueprint.co.nz

**Dr Adam Harrison B.Sc**
(1st Hons) MB BS (MD) MRCGP (2008) LL.B (Hons) Barrister-at-Law
*Diplomas in Leadership, Executive and Life Coaching; Certified Trauma-Informed Practitioner*

Adam is a former medical doctor, medical director and qualified non-practicing barrister, who specialises in wellbeing and leadership coaching and training. Specifically, he works with burning/burnt out professionals, victims and perpetrators of workplace bullying, and organisations interested in creating kinder workplace and leadership cultures.

He is also an online course creator, anti-bullying advocate, keynote speaker, and podcaster (see link below). Adam is based in Tauranga, New Zealand; however, he works across NZ, eastern Australia, UK, USA, and Canada.

www.dradamharrison.com

www.linkedin.com/in/dradamharrison

www.healthpodcastnetwork.com/show/inspiring-women-leaders

**Dr Jason Price**
**Price Perrott Limited**
Dr Jason Price is an independent specialist in workplace bullying, harassment and complaints management.

His articles, podcasts, online courses, in-person workshops, and conference speaking engagements help individuals, leadership teams and organisations who want to improve their workplace culture and complaints performance.

Price Perrott is based near Wellington, New Zealand and works with national and international clients in both public and private sectors.

www.priceperrott.com

www.linkedin.com/in/jasoneprice

Contact via: jason@priceperrott.com

**Dr Suzanne Henwood**
**mBraining4Success**
Dr Suzanne Henwood is a neuroscience-based coach and trainer who specialises in stress, anxiety, psychological safety, bullying, and heart-based leadership. She offers one on one, team coaching and workshops to support positive change. Suzanne is based in Auckland; however, she offers support globally.

www.mbraining4success.com

**Jayne Albiston**

Jayne Albiston is an independent consultant specialising in learning and professional development, stakeholder engagement, strategy, and partnerships. An international trainer, speaker and certified iMA practitioner, she is the author and developer of workshops, professional development and quality management resources and processes. Jayne has co-authored two anthologies, *I Said Yes* and *Global Women in Business*. In 2019, she compiled her first anthology, *I Said No*, featuring thirteen authors from around the globe.

Jayne is passionate about each of us realising that we are not the company brand we represent, rather we are actually our own personal brand. We owe it to ourselves to build the best version of us and to share that in the professional roles we undertake, the networks in which we grow and the relationships we build. As a survivor of workplace bullying and trauma, Jayne is on a mission to help other survivors find fresh hope and direction by rediscovering their core purpose and rebuilding an authentic personal brand to take them forward. Jayne offers one on one and group sessions and CPD (continuing professional development) workshops both on and offline. She is available for speaking/presenting at conferences or leading internal company/industry sessions for leaders and those involved with organisational and cultural change. DEI (diversity, equity and inclusion) is at the heart of Jayne's work and approach. Jayne is based in New Zealand and can support clients globally.
www.linkedin.com/in/jaynealbiston
Contact via: jaynealbiston@gmail.com

**Mental Health First Aid Aotearoa**
www.tepou.co.nz/initiatives/mental-health-first-aid-aotearoa-new-zealand
Contact via : +64 7 857 1234

# Singapore

**Kelly Kan**
**Founder & Director of Wellbeing Inside Out**
Kelly Kan is a mental wellness speaker and a professional certified coach (ICF). She founded Wellbeing Inside Out to help organisations create environments that are psychologically safe and supportive for everyone, where there is less stress, fewer burnouts and higher levels of engagement.

At Wellbeing Inside Out, the philosophy is centred on prioritising people with the belief that focusing on people first can contribute to better workplaces, where everyone feels valued, supported and empowered to reach their potential—achieving sustainable business outcomes as well as individual wellbeing.

Kelly is based in Singapore and supports clients globally as well through speaking, coaching and training.
www.wellbeinginsideout.com
Contact via: kelly.kan@wellbeinginsideout.com

**Yang Xi Ren**
**Xel Consulting Pte Ltd.**
Drawing inspiration from personal triumphs over adversities, including a traumatic experience as a survivor of alopecia areata, Xi Ren has developed a transformative yet simple framework rooted in personal experiences and backed by neuroscience to foster mental resilience.

She is passionate about empowering individuals with resilient mindsets through speeches, training and coaching so that they can thrive in challenges.
www.xelconsulting.com.sg
www.linkedin.com/in/xi-ren-yang

# United Kingdom

**Debi Roberts MA Ed**
**The OLLIE Foundation (One Life Lost is Enough)**
Debi is the CEO of The OLLIE Foundation.
The OLLIE Foundation is an expert in its field and provides a range of training for companies who want to understand how to support staff wellbeing effectively, including how to support someone returning to work following a bereavement or a mental health-related absence. Whether it's consultancy or training for staff or management, OLLIE can support your business.
www.theolliefoundation.org
Contact via: debi@theolliefoundation.org

**Jonathan Wilson LLB(Hons) BA(Hons)**
Jonathan Wilson is an Ambassador at Stop Hurt at Work. He is a Public Speaker who talks about trauma, culture, workplace, leadership and organisational behaviour.
Contact via: jonjwilson@me.com

**Nicki Eyre FRSA**
**Conduct Change Ltd**
Nicki Eyre is the managing director of Conduct Change Ltd: Better Business Behaviours through the prevention of workplace bullying.

Conduct Change provides consultancy, training and coaching solutions rooted in the prevention of workplace bullying. Their work is underpinned by their unique 3Rs Model™ - Recognise, Resolve and Recover, developed in partnership with academics and experts whose work focuses on prevention and resolution of workplace bullying.
www.conductchange.co.uk

**R;pple – the next level of suicide prevention in the workplace**
'I set up R;pple Suicide Prevention to ensure more help and support is given to individuals searching for harmful content online.'
*Alice Hendy, R;pple Founder & CEO*

R;pple is a digital crisis intervention tool designed to present a visual prompt when a person searches online for dangerous content relating to the topic of self-harm or suicide.
It provides support in three simple steps:

1. Intercepts the search with a calmly presented pop-up screen;
2. Guides the person through a filter of breathing exercises statistically proven to help them pause and reflect;
3. Signposts to helplines and mental health resources, accompanied with messages of hope.

By leveraging innovative technology, R;pple aims to ensure that immediate mental health support and resources are readily available to individuals at times when they are most vulnerable.

It helps organisations create a safer workplace, providing an additional layer of protection for employees and complementing existing mental health and wellbeing programs. Organisations can deploy R;pple en masse as a browser extension or via WiFi, while keeping user's privacy. R;pple is available globally.
www.ripplesuicideprevention.com

**Ryan Hopkins**
**JAAQ**
Ryan Hopkins is a TEDx speaker, author and the Chief Impact Officer at JAAQ. His role is about one thing and one thing only, IMPACT! With a product that changes lives, that makes workplaces a place where people can thrive, that creates a society where individuals do not need to suffer like he did, and if

they do, for them to know that they are not alone. Ryan is helping to change the world, one question at a time.

JAAQ is a new mental health social platform that is revolutionising the way people access and share information about mental health. By giving people access to world leading experts like professors, doctors and people with lived experience, they are available to answer your questions, at a touch of a button.
www.jaaq.org
linkedin.com/in/ryanhopkinsuk
Contact via: ryan@jaaq.org

## Samreen McGregor
### Executive Coach and Advisor at Turmeric and Partner of the Future Work Forum
Samreen is an executive coach whose work integrates relational, neuroscientific, psychotherapeutic, somatic, and embodied practices to support leaders in corporate contexts to make meaningful contributions—balancing performance with wellbeing. Samreen offers individual, team coaching and facilitation and advises organisations globally on how to strike a better balance between achieving desired business performance and simultaneously generating conditions for wellbeing.

Her research and interventions are targeting trauma in workplace settings. Samreen specialises in supporting C-suite leaders and executive teams, given their disproportionate influence on the organisations and communities they lead. Her book Leader *Awakened: Why accepting adversity drives power and freedom* provokes its readers to embrace healing from trauma as critical work for leading with integrity. Samreen is based in London; however, she supports businesses globally.
Contact via: admin@turmericgroup.com
www.turmericgroup.com

**Steve Carr**
**Mindcanyon: Mental health in your workplace**
Steve Carr is the founder and managing director of Mindcanyon. Mindcanyon is an award-winning mental health training service provider, offering workplace wellbeing, mental health and suicide first aid training. Mindcanyon is based in the UK; however, it support clients on a global basis.
www.mindcanyon.co.uk
Contact via: info@mindcanyon.co.uk

# United States of America

**Caroline Mrozla-Toscano, PhD**
**Trauma informed coaching**
Caroline is a leading specialist in trauma-informed approaches to workplace bullying and pedagogy and specialises in higher education. She offers consultations, training, coaching, speaking and advocacy services to promote safe and inclusive environments.
Contact via: cftoscano1@gmail.com

**Dr Gary Namie**
USA Workplace Bullying Institute
www.workplacebullying.org

**Elaine Lin Hering, JD**
Former Harvard Law School faculty, Elaine is a speaker, facilitator and author of *Unlearning Silence: How to speak your mind, unleash talent and lead with courage* (Penguin 2024). Based in the United States, Elaine works globally to support organisations in managing employee silence and building cultures of voice.
www.unlearningsilence.com
Contact via: hello@elainelinhering.com

## Mark C. Crowley
**Heart-based leadership that ignites human potential**
Mark C. Crowley is a keynote speaker, leadership consultant and Amazon best-selling author of *Lead from the Heart*. His purpose is to introduce a more scientifically informed and enlightened way of leading human beings in our workplaces, tied to his book *Lead From The Heart: Transformational Leadership For The 21st Century,* now being taught in eleven US universities. Mark provides speaking and consulting services to clients worldwide.
www.markccrowley.com
Contact via: mark@markccrowley.com

## Melissa Doman MA
**Melissa Doman LLC**
Melissa is an organisational psychologist and author of Yes, *You Can Talk About Mental Health at Work (Here's Why and How To Do It Really Well)*. Melissa Doman LLC specilises in mental health at work, navigating uncertainty, and team communication. She is based in the USA; however, she offers services to clients globally.
www.melissadoman.com

## Mental Health Innovations - North America
Mental Health Innovations (MHI) has worked with thousands of leaders from successful organizations who genuinely care about their people. These leaders strive to provide necessary support but sometimes encounter gaps in their efforts. Clients engage MHI to assist their leaders in simplifying and demystifying the complexities of mental health support.

Partnering with the MHI team means moving beyond mere lip service to mental health, fostering a culture of care that is embedded not just in policies but in the very connective tissue of an organization.

Their strategy involves action-oriented programs like implementing the WeCARE™ eLearning program for all and a specialized

WeCARE™ for Leaders. These initiatives equip leaders at all levels with the skills and courage to support those struggling with mental health issues.

As leading experts in developing and managing peer support programs, they employ a turnkey approach that leverages the lived experience of employees. This empowers employees to become pillars of support and beacons of hope for their peers. Their clientele spans various industry sectors, including healthcare, government, and first responders.

MHI has observed that organizations flourish when leaders genuinely care for the mental health of both their teams and themselves. Their commitment stands firm: rehumanising mental health in workplaces and beyond, ensuring that mental wellbeing is integral to organizational culture.
www.supportyourpeople.com
Contact via: info@mhic-cism.com

**Natasha Bowman JD, SPHR**
**The Natasha Bowman Consulting Group**
Natasha Bowman is the president of The Natasha Bowman Consulting Group. The Natasha Bowman Consulting Group brings strategic consulting, training and development programs that bridge the gap between work and wellbeing. Natasha works globally, both virtually and in person.
www.natashabowman.com

## Trauma-informed coaching

**Caroline Mrozla-Toscano, PhD**
As per details in USA section
Contact via: cftoscano1@gmail.com

**Conduct Change**
This programme supports an individual to move on after experiencing bullying in the workplace through rebuilding confidence and resilience and supporting them to step back into their own power.
www.conductchange.co.uk/moving-on

**Dr Adam Harrison B.Sc**
As per details in New Zealand section
www.dradamharrison.com

**Dr Gary Namie**
USA Workplace Bullying Institute
www.workplacebullying.org

**Dr Nathalie Martinek PhD**
As per details in Australia section
www.drnathaliemartinek.com
Contact via: hello@drnathaliemartinek.com

**Dr Suzanne Henwood**
**mBraining4Success**
As per details in New Zealand section
www.mbraining4success.com

**Felicity Menzies**
**Include-Empower**
As per details in Australia section
www.cultureplusconsulting.com

**Linda Crockett MSW, RSW, SEP, CPPA**
As per details in Canada section
www.instituteofworkplacebullyingresources.ca
www.linkedin.com/in/ciwpbr

**Samreen McGregor**
As per details in United Kingdom section
www.turmericgroup.com

**The Canadian Institute of Workplace Harassment and Violence (not for profit)**
www.workplaceharassment.ca

**The OLLIE Foundation**
The OLLIE Foundation is one of the few organisations in the world using a well-loved business tool, the Theory of Constraints, with a trauma-informed practitioner to aid personal growth and development. They also use this as a successful suicide intervention process.
www.theolliefoundation.org
Contact via: debi@theolliefoundation.org

**Traci Carse**
**TC Psychology**
As per details in Australia section
www.tcpsychology.net
Contact via: traci@tcpsychology.net

## *Mental health focused days*

Why not find out the specifc mental health focused days in your country or region, and bring the team together with a speaker on mental health? Here are some examples, but please check the dates for each year as some will change.

Australia: R U OK? Day (Second Thursday of September)
Australia: Mental Health Month (October)
New Zealand: Mental Health Awareness Week (September)

World Suicide Prevention Day (10 September)
World Mental Health Day (10 October)
Workplace Bullying Awareness Week (October)

Many countries have their own calendars for mental health awareness.

To find out what's happening in your country, you can search under these examples:

- Anti-Bullying Week
- Bullying Prevention Day
- Mental Health Month
- Mental Health Week
- Mental Health Awareness Week
- National Mental Health Day
- Stop Bullying Week
- Time to Talk Day

Lead with heart

Empathetic and encouraging

Anti-bullying and authentic

Development and diversity

Empowering and energetic

Respectful and rewarding

Safe and supportive

Honest and honourable

Inclusive and inspiring

People focused culture

# *Call to action!*

## Make a pledge to stop the bullying!

Remember, there is nothing more important than our mental health, and **creating a psychologically safe workplace is essential.**

- Ensure a zero tolerance to bullying in the workplace. Remember, your employees are human beings and you have a responsibility for a safe working environment for ALL employees.

- Define your CORE values and live and breathe them every day.

- Deep dive into what your culture REALLY looks like. Survey your staff. Ask questions and really hear the responses from your employees. Make the required change.

- Create a people focussed, safe, supportive and inclusive culture that is led from the top and embedded into the company on a day-to-day basis.

- Create a safe and inclusive workplace for people to be themselves.

- Create a safe system for people to be allowed to speak up, on any subject, with no repercussions.

- Ensure employees have satisfaction, meaning, purpose, and development in their roles.

- While culture must be led from the top, **ensure all employees know that creating a safe, supportive and inclusive culture in the workplace, is everybody's responsibility.**

- Do not create Bandaid solutions, short-term remedies or hide behind seminars, online training, apps, or just tick a box so it looks like mental health is a priority. That is only 'talking the talk'. Ensure you 'walk the walk' and follow through. These can absolutely be part of a bigger picture, but they are not the full picture.

- Watch your business and your brand thrive, and your ongoing recruitment costs decline.

Creating a mentally healthy workplace
should no longer be considered a peripheral
concern for leaders.

It is something that needs to be at the core of
successful, thriving organisations.

*Professor Samuel Harvey, Chief Scientist,
Black Dog Institute*

Building a strong culture is what builds a strong organisation.

*Simon Sinek*

A culture is strong when people work with each other, for each other.

A culture is weak when people work against each other, for themselves.

*Simon Sinek*

Leadership is a privilege. When you are in a leadership role, your influence may affect the trajectories of someone's entire career, and often their lives.

*Gifford Thomas*

When you become a leader,
you must transition from being responsible for the
job, to being responsible for the people who are
responsible for the job.

*Simon Sinek*

Leadership is not a license to do less;
it is a responsibility to do more.

*Simon Sinek*

As a leader, you should never be too busy to listen, because it's the ultimate form of respect any leader can give to their team.

*Gifford Thomas*

Leaders who check on you, listen to you and help
you grow in your career,
deserve the highest respect.

*Sibel Terhaar*

One of the essential attributes of effective leadership involves an unwavering commitment to continual learning and personal development.

*Gifford Thomas*

The greatest contribution of a leader is to make others leaders.

*Simon Sinek*

A team is not a group of people who work together. A team is a group of people who trust each other.

*Simon Sinek*

Nothing hurts more than feeling unappreciated,
undervalued and underpaid,
in a job that you love.

*Sibel Terhaar*

Leading people is a privilege, we all have an opportunity to create an environment in which every day is a great day to come to work.

*Alexander N. Andrews*

Whether you're a leader or an employee, make sure you can see the signs!

*Jo Woodhouse*

## Other books by Jo Woodhouse

**ROLLERCOASTER RIDE**

The aftermath of suicide
Poems for healing, hope
and moving forward

Jo Woodhouse

www.jowoodhouse.com

**Alison Turner PhD – Counselling Psychologist**

These beautiful and poignant poems take us on a deeply personal journey through the human repercussions of suicide. Jo walks us through a world that is often difficult to understand or comprehend and shows how the aftereffects continue to reverberate through the course of one's life and relationships. Jo plumbs the depths of grief and the heights of love with the raw honesty that only the unique and invisible wounds of suicide can produce. An exploration of the heart, trying to make sense of the unfathomable and the unwanted opportunity to recover and grow from the experience. An emotional yet therapeutic read.

## *About the author*

Jo Woodhouse lives in Sydney, Australia.

She has worked for over twenty years in the medical devices and consumables industry, but recently found the need to write about lived experiences in the hope they can help others.

Jo has had her own experiences of workplace trauma and could also see the pain others are living with all around the globe due to workplace bullying. She felt the need to write this book and try to make people see things in a different way, to reflect on their own behaviour, and to hopefully make some kind of difference in the workplace.

When Jo's not working, you will find her spending time with family and friends, with a paintbrush in hand, on long distance walks, or lazing on the beach in summer. Jo has also drafted two children's books and hopes to publish them soon.

Keep an eye on Jo's website for content updates.
www.jowoodhouse.com

## *Together, we can help stop workplace bullying!*

Remember:

We need to stand united all around the globe
Pledging to do whatever it takes
To banish workplace bullying universally
And make a psychologically safe workplace

If you were moved by this book, please share it with your leadership teams, colleagues, networks, and online communities. By spreading the word, you can empower others to speak out against bullying, create safer workplaces, and help prevent employees suffering in the future.

Together, we can help stop workplace bullying!

Thank you for being part of the solution!

www.ingramcontent.com/pod-product-compliance
Lightning Source LLC
Chambersburg PA
CBHW041157280326
41927CB00019BA/3374